Cram101 Textbook Outlines to accompany:

The Skilled Helper : A Problem Management and Opportunity Development Approach to Helping 8th

Gerard Egan, 8th Edition

A Content Technologies Inc. publication (c) 2012.

STUDYING MADE EASY

This Craml0l notebook is designed to make studying easier and increase your comprehension of the textbook material. Instead of starting with a blank notebook and trying to write down everything discussed in class lectures, you can use this Craml0l textbook notebook and annotate your notes along with the lecture.

Our goal is to give you the best tools for success.

For a supreme understanding of the course, pair your notebook with our online tools. Should you decide you prefer Craml0l.com as your study tool,

we'd like to offer you a trade...

Our Trade In program is a simple way for us to keep our promise and provide you the best studying tools, regardless of where you purchased your Craml0l textbook notebook. As long as your notebook is in *Like New Condition**, you can send it back to us and we will immediately give you a Craml0l.com account free for 120 days!

Let The *Trade In* Begin!

THREE SIMPLE STEPS TO TRADE:

1. Go to www.cram101.com/tradein and fill out the packing slip information.

2. Submit and print the packing slip and mail it in with your Craml0l textbook notebook.

3. Activate your account after you receive your email confirmation.

* Books must be returned in *Like New Condition*, meaning there is no damage to the book including, but not limited to; ripped or torn pages, markings or writing on pages, or folded / creased pages. Upon receiving the book, Craml0l will inspect it and reserves the right to terminate your free Craml0l.com account and return your textbook notebook at the owners expense.

Learning System

Cram101 Textbook Outlines is a learning system. The notes in this book are the highlights of your textbook, you will never have to highlight a book again.

How to use this book. Take this book to class, it is your notebook for the lecture. The notes and highlights on the left hand side of the pages follow the outline and order of the textbook. All you have to do is follow along while your instructor presents the lecture. Circle the items emphasized in class and add other important information on the right side. With Cram101 Textbook Outlines you'll spend less time writing and more time listening. Learning becomes more efficient.

Cram101.com Online

Increase your studying efficiency by using Cram101.com's practice tests and online reference material. It is the perfect complement to Cram101 Textbook Outlines. Use self-teaching matching tests or simulate in-class testing with comprehensive multiple choice tests, or simply use Cram's true and false tests for quick review. Cram101.com even allows you to enter your in-class notes for an integrated studying format combining the textbook notes with your class notes.

Visit **www.Cram101.com**, click Sign Up at the top of the screen, and enter **DK73DW14830** in the promo code box on the registration screen. Your access to www.Cram101.com is discounted by 50% because you have purchased this book. Sign up and stop highlighting textbooks forever.

The Skilled Helper : A Problem Management and Opportunity Development Approach to Helping 8th
Gerard Egan, 8th

CONTENTS

Chapter 1. INTRODUCTION TO HELPING

Blind spot	A blind spot, is an obscuration of the visual field. A particular blind spot known as the blindspot, or physiological blind spot, or punctum caecum in medical literature is the place in the visual field that corresponds to the lack of light-detecting photoreceptor cells on the optic disc of the retina where the optic nerve passes through it. Since there are no cells to detect light on the optic disc, a part of the field of vision is not perceived.
Resilience	Resilience is the property of a material to absorb energy when it is deformed elastically and then, upon unloading to have this energy recovered. In other words, it is the maximum energy per unit volume that can be elastically stored. It is represented by the area under the curve in the elastic region in the stress-strain curve.
Shadow	In Jungian psychology, the shadow is a part of the unconscious mind consisting of repressed weaknesses, shortcomings, and instincts. It is one of the three most recognizable archetypes, the others being the anima and animus and the persona. "Everyone carries a shadow," Jung wrote, "and the less it is embodied in the individual's conscious life, the blacker and denser it is." It may be (in part) one's link to more primitive animal instincts, which are superseded during early childhood by the conscious mind.
Life skills	Life skills are a set of human skills acquired via teaching or direct experience that are used to handle problems and questions commonly encountered in daily human life.
Emotional intelligence	Emotional intelligence is the ability, capacity, skill; or, in the case of the trait Emotional intelligence model, a self-perceived ability to identify, assess, and control the emotions of oneself, of others, and of groups. Different models have been proposed for the definition of Emotional intelligence and there is disagreement about how the term should be used. Despite these disagreements, which are often highly technical, the ability-Emotional intelligence and trait-Emotional intelligence models (but not the mixed models) enjoy support in the literature and have successful applications in various domains.
Epistemology	Epistemology is the branch of philosophy concerned with the nature and scope (limitations) of knowledge. It addresses the questions: • What is knowledge? • How is knowledge acquired? • How do we know what we know?

Go to **Cram101.com** for Interactive Practice Exams for this book or virtually any of your books.
And, **NEVER** highlight a book again!

Chapter 1. INTRODUCTION TO HELPING

In physics, the concept of epistemology is vital in the modern interpretation of quantum mechanics, and is used by many authors to analyse the works of dominant physicists such as Werner Heisenberg, Max Born and Wolfgang Pauli.

Much of the debate in this field has focused on analyzing the nature of knowledge and how it relates to connected notions such as truth, belief, and justification.

Positivism

Positivism refers to a set of epistemological perspectives and philosophies of science which hold that the scientific method is the best approach to uncovering the processes by which both physical and human events occur. Though the positivist approach has been a 'recurrent theme in the history of western thought from the Ancient Greeks to the present day' the concept was developed in the early 19th century by the philosopher and founding sociologist, Auguste Comte.

Overview

Positivism asserts that the only authentic knowledge is that which is based on sense, experience and positive verification.

Self-awareness

Self-awareness is the awareness that one exists as an individual being. Without self-awareness the self perceives and accepts the thoughts that are occurring to be who the self is. Self-awareness gives one the option or choice to choose thoughts being thought rather than simply thinking the thoughts that are stimulated from the accumulative events leading up to the circumstances of the moment.

Communication

Communication is a process whereby meaning is defined and shared between living organisms. Communication requires a sender, a message, and an intended recipient, although the receiver need not be present or aware of the sender's intent to communicate at the time of communication; thus communication can occur across vast distances in time and space. Communication requires that the communicating parties share an area of communicative commonality.

Chapter 1. INTRODUCTION TO HELPING

Constructivism	Constructivism in Psychology concerns the world of constructivist psychologies. Many schools of psychotherapy self-define themselves as "constructivist". Although extraordinarily different in their therapeutic techniques, they are all connected by a common critique to previous standard approaches and by shared assumptions about the constructive nature of knowledge.
Empathy	Empathy is the capacity to recognize and, to some extent, share feelings (such as sadness or happiness) that are being experienced by another semi-sentient being. Someone may need to have a certain amount of empathy before they are able to feel compassion. Etymology The English word is derived from the Greek word ?μπ?θεια (empatheia), "physical affection, passion, partiality" which comes from ?ν (en), "in, at" + π?θος (pathos), "passion" or "suffering".
Interpersonal relationship	An interpersonal relationship is an association between two or more people that may range from fleeting to enduring. This association may be based on limerence, love, solidarity, regular business interactions, or some other type of social commitment. Interpersonal relationships are formed in the context of social, cultural and other influences.
Psychologist	Psychologist is an academic, occupational or professional title used by individuals who are either: • Social scientists conducting psychological research or teaching psychology in a college or university; • Academic professionals who apply psychological research, theories and techniques to "real-world" problems, questions and issues in business, industry, or government. • Clinical professionals who work with patients in a variety of therapeutic contexts (contrast with psychiatrists, who typically provide medical interventions and drug therapies, as opposed to analysis and counseling).

Chapter 1. INTRODUCTION TO HELPING

There are many different types of psychologists, as is reflected by the 56 different divisions of the American Psychological Association (APA). Psychologists are generally described as being either "applied" or "research-oriented". The common terms used to describe this central division in psychology are "scientists" or "scholars" (those who conduct research) and "practitioners" or "professionals" (those who apply psychological knowledge).

Active

ACTIVE - sobriety, friendship and peace (formerly EGTYF, European Good Templar Youth Federation) is a non-governmental umbrella organisation gathering European youth temperance organisations. ACTIVE is member of the Youth Forum Jeunesse and cooperates with IOGT International.

The main aim of Active is peace and tolerance in the world.

Active listening

Active listening is a communication technique that requires the listener to understand, interpret, and evaluate what (s)he hears. The ability to listen actively can improve personal relationships through reducing conflicts, strengthening cooperation, and fostering understanding.

When interacting, people often are not listening attentively.

Counseling Psychology

Counseling psychology is a psychological specialty that encompasses research and applied work in several broad domains: counseling process and outcome; supervision and training; career development and counseling; and prevention and health. Some unifying themes among counseling psychologists include a focus on assets and strengths, person-environment interactions development, brief interactions, and a focus on intact personalities. In the United States, the premier scholarly journals of the profession are the Journal of Counseling Psychology and The Counseling Psychologist.

Chapter 1. INTRODUCTION TO HELPING

Evidence-based practice	The term evidence-based practice or empirically-supported treatment (EST) refers to preferential use of mental and behavioral health interventions for which systematic empirical research has provided evidence of statistically significant effectiveness as treatments for specific problems. In recent years, Evidence based practice has been stressed by professional organizations such as the American Psychological Association, the American Occupational Therapy Association, the American Nurses Association, and the American Physical Therapy Association, which have also strongly recommended their members to carry out investigations to provide evidence supporting or rejecting the use of specific interventions. Equivalent recommendations apply to the Canadian equivalent of these associations.
Qualitative research	Qualitative research is a method of inquiry employed in many different academic disciplines, traditionally in the social sciences, but also in market research and further contexts. Qualitative researchers aim to gather an in-depth understanding of human behavior and the reasons that govern such behavior. The qualitative method investigates the why and how of decision making, not just what, where, when.
Sampling	Sampling is that part of statistical practice concerned with the selection of a subset of individual observations within a population of individuals intended to yield some knowledge about the population of concern, especially for the purposes of making predictions based on statistical inference.
	Researchers rarely survey the entire population for two reasons (Adèr, Mellenbergh, ' Hand, 2008): the cost is too high, and the population is dynamic in that the individuals making up the population may change over time. The three main advantages of sampling are that the cost is lower, data collection is faster, and since the data set is smaller it is possible to ensure homogeneity and to improve the accuracy and quality of the data.
Science	Science is an enterprise that builds and organizes knowledge in the form of testable explanations and predictions about the world. An older meaning still in use today is that of Aristotle, for whom scientific knowledge was a body of reliable knowledge that can be logically and rationally explained .
	Since classical antiquity science as a type of knowledge was closely linked to philosophy.

Chapter 1. INTRODUCTION TO HELPING

Scientific method	Scientific method refers to a body of techniques for investigating phenomena, acquiring new knowledge, or correcting and integrating previous knowledge. To be termed scientific, a method of inquiry must be based on gathering observable, empirical and measurable evidence subject to specific principles of reasoning. The Oxford English Dictionary says that scientific method is: "a method of procedure that has characterized natural science since the 17th century, consisting in systematic observation, measurement, and experiment, and the formulation, testing, and modification of hypotheses." Although procedures vary from one field of inquiry to another, identifiable features distinguish scientific inquiry from other methods of obtaining knowledge.
Research	Research can be defined as the search for knowledge, or as any systematic investigation, with an open mind, to establish novel facts, usually using a scientific method. The primary purpose for applied research is discovering, interpreting, and the development of methods and systems for the advancement of human knowledge on a wide variety of scientific matters of our world and the universe. Scientific research relies on the application of the scientific method, a harnessing of curiosity.
Incentive	In economics and sociology, an incentive is any factor (financial or non-financial) that enables or motivates a particular course of action, or counts as a reason for preferring one choice to the alternatives. It is an expectation that encourages people to behave in a certain way. Since human beings are purposeful creatures, the study of incentive structures is central to the study of all economic activity (both in terms of individual decision-making and in terms of co-operation and competition within a larger institutional structure).
Clinical Psychology	Clinical psychology is an integration of science, theory and clinical knowledge for the purpose of understanding, preventing, and relieving psychologically based distress or dysfunction and to promote subjective well-being and personal development. Central to its practice are psychological assessment and psychological treatment, although clinical psychologists also engage in research, teaching, consultation, forensic testimony, and program development and administration. In many countries, clinical psychology is a regulated mental health profession.

Chapter 1. INTRODUCTION TO HELPING

Journal of Clinical Psychology	The Journal of Clinical Psychology, founded in 1945, is a peer-reviewed forum devoted to psychological research, assessment, and practice. Published eight times a year, the Journal includes research studies; articles on contemporary professional issues, single case research; brief reports (including dissertations in brief); notes from the field; and news and notes. In addition to papers on psychopathology, psychodiagnostics, and the psychotherapeutic process, the journal welcomes articles focusing on psychotherapy effectiveness research, psychological assessment and treatment matching, clinical outcomes, clinical health psychology, and behavioral medicine.
Hunch	Hunch is a website, designed as a collective intelligence decision-making system that uses decision trees to make decisions based on users' interest. Hunch is building the 'taste graph' for the internet, mapping every person to every entity -- and their affinity for that entity. The system asks users a series of questions about a topic to help weigh the options.
Positive Psychology	Positive psychology is a recent branch of psychology whose purpose was summed up in 2000 by Martin Seligman and Mihaly Csikszentmihalyi: "We believe that a psychology of positive human functioning will arise that achieves a scientific understanding and effective interventions to build thriving in individuals, families, and communities." Positive psychologists seek "to find and nurture genius and talent", and "to make normal life more fulfilling", not simply to treat mental illness. The emerging field of Positive Psychology is intended to complement, not to replace traditional psychology. By scientifically studying what has gone right, rather than wrong in both individuals and societies, Positive Psychology hopes to achieve a renaissance of sorts.
Curriculum	In formal education, a curriculum is the set of courses, and their content, offered at a school or university. As an idea, curriculum stems from the Latin word for race course, referring to the course of deeds and experiences through which children grow to become mature adults. A curriculum is prescriptive, and is based on a more general syllabus which merely specifies what topics must be understood and to what level to achieve a particular grade or standard.

Chapter 1. INTRODUCTION TO HELPING

Developmental psychology	Developmental psychology, is the scientific study of systematic psychological changes that occur in human beings over the course of their life span. Originally concerned with infants and children, the field has expanded to include adolescence, adult development, aging, and the entire life span. This field examines change across a broad range of topics including motor skills and other psycho-physiological processes; cognitive development involving areas such as problem solving, moral understanding, and conceptual understanding; language acquisition; social, personality, and emotional development; and self-concept and identity formation.
Knowledge	Knowledge is defined by the Oxford English Dictionary as (i) expertise, and skills acquired by a person through experience or education; the theoretical or practical understanding of a subject; (ii) what is known in a particular field or in total; facts and information; or (iii) be absolutely certain or sure about something. Philosophical debates in general start with Plato's formulation of knowledge as "justified true belief." There is however no single agreed definition of knowledge presently, nor any prospect of one, and there remain numerous competing theories. Knowledge acquisition involves complex cognitive processes: perception, learning, communication, association and reasoning.
Common sense	Common sense, based on a strict construction of the term, consists of what people in common would agree on : that which they "sense" as their common natural understanding. Some people (such as the authors of Merriam-Webster Online) use the phrase to refer to beliefs or propositions that -- in their opinion -- most people would consider prudent and of sound judgment, without reliance on esoteric knowledge or study or research, but based upon what they see as knowledge held by people "in common". Thus "common sense" (in this view) equates to the knowledge and experience which most people already have, or which the person using the term believes that they do or should have.
Model	Art models are models who pose for photographers, painters, sculptors, and other artists as part of their work of art. Art models are often paid, sometimes even professional, human subjects, who aid in creating a portrait or other work of art including such figure wholly or partially. Models are frequently used for training art students, but are also employed by accomplished artists.

Chapter 1. INTRODUCTION TO HELPING

Perspective	Perspective, in context of vision and visual perception, is the way in which objects appear to the eye based on their spatial attributes; or their dimensions and the position of the eye relative to the objects. There are two main meanings of the term: linear perspective and aerial perspective. Linear perspective As objects become more distant they appear smaller because their visual angle decreases.
Strategies for Engineered Negligible Senescence	Strategies for Engineered Negligible Senescence is the name Aubrey de Grey gives to his proposal to research regenerative medical procedures to periodically repair all the age-related damage in the human body, thereby maintaining a youthful state indefinitely SENS has received media attention but has been criticized by some scientists.
Wisdom	Wisdom is a deep understanding and realizing of people, things, events or situations, resulting in the ability to choose or act to consistently produce the optimum results with a minimum of time and energy. It is the ability to optimally (effectively and efficiently) apply perceptions and knowledge and so produce the desired results. Wisdom is also the comprehension of what is true or right coupled with optimum judgment as to action.
Hope	Hope is the belief in a positive outcome related to events and circumstances in one's life. Hope is distinct from positive thinking, which refers to a therapeutic or systematic process used in psychology for reversing pessimism. The term false hope refers to a hope based entirely around a fantasy or an extremely unlikely outcome.
Human behavior	Human behavior is the population of behaviors exhibited by humans and influenced by culture, attitudes, emotions, values, ethics, authority, rapport, hypnosis, persuasion, coercion and/or genetics.

Chapter 1. INTRODUCTION TO HELPING

The behavior of people (and other organisms or even mechanisms) falls within a range with some behavior being common, some unusual, some acceptable, and some outside acceptable limits. In sociology, behavior is considered as having social behavior, which is more advanced action, as social behavior is behavior specifically directed at other people.

Personality psychology	Personality psychology is a branch of psychology that studies personality and individual differences. Its areas of focus include: • Constructing a coherent picture of a person and his or her major psychological processes • Investigating individual differences, that is, how people can differ from one another. • Investigating human nature, that is, how all people's behaviour is similar. Personality can be defined as a dynamic and organized set of characteristics possessed by a person that uniquely influences his or her cognitions, motivations, and behaviors in various situations. The word "personality" originates from the Latin persona, which means mask.
Social psychology	Social psychology is the scientific study of how people's thoughts, feelings, and behaviors are influenced by the actual, imagined, or implied presence of others. By this definition, scientific refers to the empirical method of investigation. The terms thoughts, feelings, and behaviors include all of the psychological variables that are measurable in a human being.
Divergent thinking	Divergent thinking is a thought process or method used to generate creative ideas by exploring many possible solutions. It is often used in conjunction with convergent thinking, which follows a particular set of logical steps to arrive at one solution, which in some cases is a "correct" solution. Divergent thinking typically occurs in a spontaneous, free-flowing manner, such that many ideas are generated in an unorganized fashion.
Burnout	Burnout is a psychological term for the experience of long-term exhaustion and diminished interest. Research indicates general practitioners have the highest proportion of burnout cases (according to a recent Dutch study in Psychological Reports, no less than 40% of these experienced high levels of burnout). Burnout is not a recognized disorder in the DSM although it is recognized in the ICD-10 as "Problems related to life-management difficulty".

Chapter 1. INTRODUCTION TO HELPING

Spirituality	Spirituality can refer to an ultimate or immaterial reality; an inner path enabling a person to discover the essence of their being; or the "deepest values and meanings by which people live." Spiritual practices, including meditation, prayer and contemplation, are intended to develop an individual's inner life; such practices often lead to an experience of connectedness with a larger reality, yielding a more comprehensive self; with other individuals or the human community; with nature or the cosmos; or with the divine realm. Spirituality is often experienced as a source of inspiration or orientation in life. It can encompass belief in immaterial realities or experiences of the immanent or transcendent nature of the world.
Forensic psychology	Forensic psychology is the intersection between psychology and the criminal justice system. It involves understanding criminal law in the relevant jurisdictions in order to be able to interact appropriately with judges, attorneys and other legal professionals. An important aspect of forensic psychology is the ability to testify in court, reformulating psychological findings into the legal language of the courtroom, providing information to legal personnel in a way that can be understood.
Stochastic resonance	Stochastic resonance is a phenomenon that occurs in a threshold measurement system (e.g. a man-made instrument or device; a natural cell, organ or organism) when an appropriate measure of information transfer (signal-to-noise ratio, mutual information, coherence, d, etc). is maximized in the presence of a non-zero level of stochastic input noise thereby lowering the response threshold; the system resonates at a particular noise level. Stochastic resonance is observed when noise added to a system changes the system's behaviour in some fashion.
Critical Thinking	Critical thinking, in its broadest sense has been described as "purposeful reflective judgment concerning what to believe or what to do." Meaning Critical thinking clarifies goals, examines assumptions, discerns hidden values, evaluates evidence, accomplishes actions, and assesses conclusions.

"Critical" as used in the expression "critical thinking" connotes the importance or centrality of the thinking to an issue, question or problem of concern. "Critical" in this context does not mean "disapproval" or "negative." There are many positive and useful uses of critical thinking, for example formulating a workable solution to a complex personal problem, deliberating as a group about what course of action to take, or analyzing the assumptions and the quality of the methods used in scientifically arriving at a reasonable level of confidence about a given hypothesis.

Therapeutic relationship	The therapeutic relationship, the therapeutic alliance, and the working alliance, refers to the relationship between a healthcare professional and a client (or patient). It is the means by which the professional hopes to engage with, and affect change in a client.

Research

While much early work on this subject was generated from a psychodynamic perspective, researchers from other orientations have since investigated this area.

Chapter 2. OVERVIEW OF THE HELPING MODEL

Blind spot	A blind spot, is an obscuration of the visual field. A particular blind spot known as the blindspot, or physiological blind spot, or punctum caecum in medical literature is the place in the visual field that corresponds to the lack of light-detecting photoreceptor cells on the optic disc of the retina where the optic nerve passes through it. Since there are no cells to detect light on the optic disc, a part of the field of vision is not perceived.
Problem solving	Problem solving is a mental process and is part of the larger problem process that includes problem finding and problem shaping. Considered the most complex of all intellectual functions, problem solving has been defined as higher-order cognitive process that requires the modulation and control of more routine or fundamental skills. Problem solving occurs when an organism or an artificial intelligence system needs to move from a given state to a desired goal state.
Contemplation	The word contemplation comes from the Latin word contemplatio. Its root is also that of the Latin word templum, a piece of ground consecrated for the taking of auspices, or a building for worship, derived either from Proto-Indo-European base *tem- "to cut", and so a "place reserved or cut out" or from the Proto-Indo-European base *temp- "to stretch", and thus referring to a cleared space in front of an altar. The Latin word contemplatio was used to translated the Greek word θεωρ?α (theoria).
Empowerment	Empowerment refers to increasing the spiritual, political, social, or economic strength of individuals and communities. It often involves the empowered developing confidence in their own capacities.
Decision making	Decision making can be regarded as the mental processes (cognitive process) resulting in the selection of a course of action among several alternatives. Every decision making process produces a final choice. The output can be an action or an opinion of choice.
Storytelling	Storytelling is the conveying of events in words, images and sounds, often by improvisation or embellishment. Stories or narratives have been shared in every culture as a means of entertainment, education, cultural preservation and in order to instill moral values. Crucial elements of stories and storytelling include plot, characters and narrative point of view.
Leverage	In statistics, leverage is a term used in connection with regression analysis and, in particular, in analyses aimed at identifying those observations which have a large effect on the outcome of fitting regression models.

Chapter 2. OVERVIEW OF THE HELPING MODEL

	Leverage points are those observations, if any, made at extreme or outlying values of the independent variables such that the lack of neighbouring observations means that the fitted regression model will pass close to that particular observation. Modern computer packages for statistical analysis include, as part of their facilities for regression analysis, various quantitative measures for identifying influential observations: among these measures is partial leverage, a measure of how a variable contributes to the leverage of a datum.
Model	Art models are models who pose for photographers, painters, sculptors, and other artists as part of their work of art. Art models are often paid, sometimes even professional, human subjects, who aid in creating a portrait or other work of art including such figure wholly or partially. Models are frequently used for training art students, but are also employed by accomplished artists.
Affect	"Affect" is a concept used in philosophy by Spinoza, Deleuze and Guattari. According to Spinoza's Ethics III, 3, Definition 3, an affect is an empowerment, and not a simple change or modification. Affects, according to Deleuze, are not simple affections, as they are independent from their subject.
Agenda	An agenda is a list of meeting activities in the order in which they are to be taken up, beginning with the call to order and ending with adjournment. It usually includes one or more specific items of business to be considered. It may, but is not required to, include specific times for one OR more activities.
Self-disclosure	Self-disclosure is both the conscious and unconscious act of revealing more about oneself to others. This may include, but is not limited to, thoughts, feelings, aspirations, goals, failures, successes, fears, dreams as well as one's likes, dislikes, and favorites.

29

Typically, a self-disclosure happens when we initially meet someone and continues as we build and develop our relationships with people. As we get to know each other, we disclose information about ourselves. If one person is not willing to "self-disclose" then the other person may stop disclosing information about themselves as well.

Shaping	The differential reinforcement of successive approximations, or more commonly, shaping is a conditioning procedure used primarily in the experimental analysis of behavior. It was introduced by B.F. Skinner with pigeons and extended to dogs, dolphins, humans and other species. In shaping, the form of an existing response is gradually changed across successive trials towards a desired target behavior by rewarding exact segments of behavior.
Coercion	Coercion is the practice of forcing another party to behave in an involuntary manner (whether through action or inaction) by use of threats,or rewards intimidation or some other form of pressure or force. Such actions are used as leverage, to force the victim to act in the desired way. Coercion may involve the actual infliction of physical pain/injury or psychological harm in order to enhance the credibility of a threat.
Cognitive dissonance	Cognitive dissonance is an uncomfortable feeling caused by holding conflicting ideas simultaneously. The theory of cognitive dissonance proposes that people have a motivational drive to reduce dissonance. They do this by changing their attitudes, beliefs, and actions.
Cognitive psychology	Cognitive psychology is a subdiscipline of psychology exploring internal mental processes. It is the study of how people perceive, remember, think, speak, and solve problems. Cognitive psychology is radically different from previous psychological approaches in two key ways.
Shadow	In Jungian psychology, the shadow is a part of the unconscious mind consisting of repressed weaknesses, shortcomings, and instincts. It is one of the three most recognizable archetypes, the others being the anima and animus and the persona. "Everyone carries a shadow," Jung wrote, "and the less it is embodied in the individual's conscious life, the blacker and denser it is." It may be (in part) one's link to more primitive animal instincts, which are superseded during early childhood by the conscious mind.

Chapter 2. OVERVIEW OF THE HELPING MODEL

Rating Scale	A rating scale is a set of categorize designed to elicit information about a quantitative or a qualitative attribute. In the social sciences, common examples are the Likert scale and 1-10 rating scales in which a person selects the number which is considered to reflect the perceived quality of a product. A rating scale is an instrument that requires the rater to assign the rated object that have numerals assigned to them.
Human universals	Human Universals is a book by Donald Brown, an American professor of anthropology (emeritus) who worked at the University of California, Santa Barbara. It was published by McGraw Hill in 1991. The book argues against cultural relativism, which was the dominant approach in many social sciences in the late twentieth century. Brown says human universals, "comprise those features of culture, society, language, behavior, and psyche for which there are no known exception." He is quoted at length by Steven Pinker in an appendix to The Blank Slate, where Pinker cites some of the hundreds of universals listed by Brown.
Understanding	Understanding is a psychological process related to an abstract or physical object, such as a person, situation, or message whereby one is able to think about it and use concepts to deal adequately with that object. An understanding is the limit of a conceptualization. To understand something is to have conceptualized it to a given measure.
Rigidity	In psychology, rigidity refers to an obstinate inability to yield. A refusal to appreciate another person's viewpoint or emotions, characterized by a lack of empathy. A specific example is functional fixedness, which is a difficulty conceiving new uses for familiar objects.

Chapter 3. THE HELPING RELATIONSHIP: VALUES IN ACTION

Common sense	Common sense, based on a strict construction of the term, consists of what people in common would agree on : that which they "sense" as their common natural understanding. Some people (such as the authors of Merriam-Webster Online) use the phrase to refer to beliefs or propositions that -- in their opinion -- most people would consider prudent and of sound judgment, without reliance on esoteric knowledge or study or research, but based upon what they see as knowledge held by people "in common". Thus "common sense" (in this view) equates to the knowledge and experience which most people already have, or which the person using the term believes that they do or should have.
Model	Art models are models who pose for photographers, painters, sculptors, and other artists as part of their work of art. Art models are often paid, sometimes even professional, human subjects, who aid in creating a portrait or other work of art including such figure wholly or partially. Models are frequently used for training art students, but are also employed by accomplished artists.
Strategies for Engineered Negligible Senescence	Strategies for Engineered Negligible Senescence is the name Aubrey de Grey gives to his proposal to research regenerative medical procedures to periodically repair all the age-related damage in the human body, thereby maintaining a youthful state indefinitely SENS has received media attention but has been criticized by some scientists.
Shadow	In Jungian psychology, the shadow is a part of the unconscious mind consisting of repressed weaknesses, shortcomings, and instincts. It is one of the three most recognizable archetypes, the others being the anima and animus and the persona. "Everyone carries a shadow," Jung wrote, "and the less it is embodied in the individual's conscious life, the blacker and denser it is." It may be (in part) one's link to more primitive animal instincts, which are superseded during early childhood by the conscious mind.

Chapter 3. THE HELPING RELATIONSHIP: VALUES IN ACTION

Wisdom	Wisdom is a deep understanding and realizing of people, things, events or situations, resulting in the ability to choose or act to consistently produce the optimum results with a minimum of time and energy. It is the ability to optimally (effectively and efficiently) apply perceptions and knowledge and so produce the desired results. Wisdom is also the comprehension of what is true or right coupled with optimum judgment as to action.
Transference	Transference is a phenomenon in psychoanalysis characterized by unconscious redirection of feelings from one person to another. One definition of transference is "the inappropriate repetition in the present of a relationship that was important in a person's childhood." Another definition is "the redirection of feelings and desires and especially of those unconsciously retained from childhood toward a new object." Still another definition is "a reproduction of emotions relating to repressed experiences, esp[ecially] of childhood, and the substitution of another person ... for the original object of the repressed impulses." Transference was first described by Sigmund Freud, who acknowledged its importance for psychoanalysis for better understanding of the patient's feelings.

Occurrence

It is common for people to transfer feelings from their parents to their partners or children (i.e., cross-generational entanglements). |
| Active | ACTIVE - sobriety, friendship and peace (formerly EGTYF, European Good Templar Youth Federation) is a non-governmental umbrella organisation gathering European youth temperance organisations. ACTIVE is member of the Youth Forum Jeunesse and cooperates with IOGT International.

The main aim of Active is peace and tolerance in the world. |
| Active listening | Active listening is a communication technique that requires the listener to understand, interpret, and evaluate what (s)he hears. The ability to listen actively can improve personal relationships through reducing conflicts, strengthening cooperation, and fostering understanding. |

Chapter 3. THE HELPING RELATIONSHIP: VALUES IN ACTION

	When interacting, people often are not listening attentively.
Flexibility	Flexibility is a personality trait -- the extent to which a person can cope with changes in circumstances and think about problems and tasks in novel, creative ways.
Learning	Learning is acquiring new or modifying existing knowledge, behaviors, skills, values, or preferences and may involve synthesizing different types of information. The ability to learn is possessed by humans, animals and some machines. Progress over time tends to follow learning curves.
Goal setting	Goal setting involves establishing specific, measurable and time-targeted objectives. Goal setting features as a major component of personal development literature. Goals perceived as realistic are more effective in changing behavior.
Belief	Belief is the psychological state in which an individual holds a proposition or premise to be true.

Belief, knowledge and epistemology

The terms belief and knowledge are used differently in philosophy.

Epistemology is the philosophical study of knowledge and belief. |
| Respect | Respect denotes both a positive feeling of esteem for a person of other entity (such as a nation or a religion), and also specific actions and conduct representative of that esteem. Respect can be a specific feeling of regard for the actual qualities of the one respected (e.g., "I have great respect for her judgment"). It can also be conduct in accord with a specific ethic of respect. |
| Empathy | Empathy is the capacity to recognize and, to some extent, share feelings (such as sadness or happiness) that are being experienced by another semi-sentient being. Someone may need to have a certain amount of empathy before they are able to feel compassion.

Etymology |

The English word is derived from the Greek word ?μπ?θεια (empatheia), "physical affection, passion, partiality" which comes from ?v (en), "in, at" + π?θος (pathos), "passion" or "suffering".

Psychologist	Psychologist is an academic, occupational or professional title used by individuals who are either:

- Social scientists conducting psychological research or teaching psychology in a college or university;
- Academic professionals who apply psychological research, theories and techniques to "real-world" problems, questions and issues in business, industry, or government.
- Clinical professionals who work with patients in a variety of therapeutic contexts (contrast with psychiatrists, who typically provide medical interventions and drug therapies, as opposed to analysis and counseling).

There are many different types of psychologists, as is reflected by the 56 different divisions of the American Psychological Association (APA). Psychologists are generally described as being either "applied" or "research-oriented". The common terms used to describe this central division in psychology are "scientists" or "scholars" (those who conduct research) and "practitioners" or "professionals" (those who apply psychological knowledge).

Agenda	An agenda is a list of meeting activities in the order in which they are to be taken up, beginning with the call to order and ending with adjournment. It usually includes one or more specific items of business to be considered. It may, but is not required to, include specific times for one OR more activities.
Facilitation	Facilitation in business, organizational development (OD) and in consensus decision-making refers to the process of designing and running a successful meeting.

Facilitation concerns itself with all the tasks needed to run a productive and impartial meeting. Facilitation serves the needs of any group who are meeting with a common purpose, whether it be making a decision, solving a problem, or simply exchanging ideas and information.

Clam101

Chapter 3. THE HELPING RELATIONSHIP: VALUES IN ACTION

Empowerment

Empowerment refers to increasing the spiritual, political, social, or economic strength of individuals and communities. It often involves the empowered developing confidence in their own capacities.

Resilience

Resilience is the property of a material to absorb energy when it is deformed elastically and then, upon unloading to have this energy recovered. In other words, it is the maximum energy per unit volume that can be elastically stored. It is represented by the area under the curve in the elastic region in the stress-strain curve.

Resistance

"Resistance" as initially used by Sigmund Freud, referred to patients blocking memories from conscious memory. This was a key concept, since the primary treatment method of Freud's talk therapy required making these memories available to the patient's consciousness.

"Resistance" expanded

Later, Freud described five different forms of resistance.

Conscientiousness

Conscientiousness has many definitions. One is awareness, others are the trait of being painstaking and careful, or the quality of acting according to the dictates of one's conscience. It includes such elements as self-discipline, carefulness, thoroughness, organization, deliberation (the tendency to think carefully before acting), and need for achievement.

Bias

In statistics, the term bias refers to several different concepts:

- Selection bias, where individuals or groups are more likely to take part in a research project than others, resulting in biased samples. This can also be termed Berksonian bias.
  - Spectrum bias arises from evaluating diagnostic tests on biased patient samples, leading to an overestimate of the sensitivity and specificity of the test.
- The bias of an estimator is the difference between an estimator's expectation and the true value of the parameter being estimated.

Chapter 3. THE HELPING RELATIONSHIP: VALUES IN ACTION

Divergent thinking	Divergent thinking is a thought process or method used to generate creative ideas by exploring many possible solutions. It is often used in conjunction with convergent thinking, which follows a particular set of logical steps to arrive at one solution, which in some cases is a "correct" solution. Divergent thinking typically occurs in a spontaneous, free-flowing manner, such that many ideas are generated in an unorganized fashion.
Collaboration	Collaboration is a recursive process where two or more people or organizations work together to realize shared goals, -- for example, an intruiging endeavor that is creative in nature--by sharing knowledge, learning and building consensus. Most collaboration requires leadership, although the form of leadership can be social within a decentralized and egalitarian group. In particular, teams that work collaboratively can obtain greater resources, recognition and reward when facing competition for finite resources.
Blind spot	A blind spot, is an obscuration of the visual field. A particular blind spot known as the blindspot, or physiological blind spot, or punctum caecum in medical literature is the place in the visual field that corresponds to the lack of light-detecting photoreceptor cells on the optic disc of the retina where the optic nerve passes through it. Since there are no cells to detect light on the optic disc, a part of the field of vision is not perceived.

Chapter 4. COMMUNICATION

Active	ACTIVE - sobriety, friendship and peace (formerly EGTYF, European Good Templar Youth Federation) is a non-governmental umbrella organisation gathering European youth temperance organisations. ACTIVE is member of the Youth Forum Jeunesse and cooperates with IOGT International. The main aim of Active is peace and tolerance in the world.
Active listening	Active listening is a communication technique that requires the listener to understand, interpret, and evaluate what (s)he hears. The ability to listen actively can improve personal relationships through reducing conflicts, strengthening cooperation, and fostering understanding. When interacting, people often are not listening attentively.
Blind spot	A blind spot, is an obscuration of the visual field. A particular blind spot known as the blindspot, or physiological blind spot, or punctum caecum in medical literature is the place in the visual field that corresponds to the lack of light-detecting photoreceptor cells on the optic disc of the retina where the optic nerve passes through it. Since there are no cells to detect light on the optic disc, a part of the field of vision is not perceived.
Creativity	Creativity refers to the phenomenon whereby a person creates something new (a product, a solution, a work of art etc). that has some kind of value. What counts as "new" may be in reference to the individual creator, or to the society or domain within which the novelty occurs.
Self-disclosure	Self-disclosure is both the conscious and unconscious act of revealing more about oneself to others. This may include, but is not limited to, thoughts, feelings, aspirations, goals, failures, successes, fears, dreams as well as one's likes, dislikes, and favorites. Typically, a self-disclosure happens when we initially meet someone and continues as we build and develop our relationships with people. As we get to know each other, we disclose information about ourselves. If one person is not willing to "self-disclose" then the other person may stop disclosing information about themselves as well.

Chapter 4. COMMUNICATION

Communication	Communication is a process whereby meaning is defined and shared between living organisms. Communication requires a sender, a message, and an intended recipient, although the receiver need not be present or aware of the sender's intent to communicate at the time of communication; thus communication can occur across vast distances in time and space. Communication requires that the communicating parties share an area of communicative commonality.
Facial expression	A facial expression results from one or more motions or positions of the muscles of the face. These movements convey the emotional state of the individual to observers. Facial expressions are a form of nonverbal communication.
Health	Health is the general condition of a person in all aspects. It is also a level of functional and/or metabolic efficiency of an organism, often implicitly human. "The state of being free from illness or injury".
Mental Health	Mental health describes either a level of cognitive or emotional well-being or an absence of a mental disorder. From perspectives of the discipline of positive psychology or holism mental health may include an individual's ability to enjoy life and procure a balance between life activities and efforts to achieve psychological resilience. Mental health is an expression of our emotions and signifies a successful adaptation to a range of demands.
Decision making	Decision making can be regarded as the mental processes (cognitive process) resulting in the selection of a course of action among several alternatives. Every decision making process produces a final choice. The output can be an action or an opinion of choice.
Anger	Anger is an emotion related to one's psychological interpretation of having been offended, wronged or denied and a tendency to undo that by retaliation. Videbeck describes anger as a normal emotion that involves a strong uncomfortable and emotional response to a perceived provocation. R. Novaco recognized three modalities of anger: cognitive (appraisals), somatic-affective (tension and agitations) and behavioral (withdrawal and antagonism).
Anger management	The term anger management commonly refers to a system of psychological therapeutic techniques and exercises by which someone with excessive or uncontrollable anger can control or reduce the triggers, degrees, and effects of an angered emotional state. In some countries, courses in anger management may be mandated by their legal system.
	One strategy for controlling anger is finding agreement with another person rather than conflict.

Chapter 4. COMMUNICATION

Clinical Psychology	Clinical psychology is an integration of science, theory and clinical knowledge for the purpose of understanding, preventing, and relieving psychologically based distress or dysfunction and to promote subjective well-being and personal development. Central to its practice are psychological assessment and psychological treatment, although clinical psychologists also engage in research, teaching, consultation, forensic testimony, and program development and administration. In many countries, clinical psychology is a regulated mental health profession.
Journal of Clinical Psychology	The Journal of Clinical Psychology, founded in 1945, is a peer-reviewed forum devoted to psychological research, assessment, and practice. Published eight times a year, the Journal includes research studies; articles on contemporary professional issues, single case research; brief reports (including dissertations in brief); notes from the field; and news and notes. In addition to papers on psychopathology, psychodiagnostics, and the psychotherapeutic process, the journal welcomes articles focusing on psychotherapy effectiveness research, psychological assessment and treatment matching, clinical outcomes, clinical health psychology, and behavioral medicine.
Identification	Identification is a psychological process whereby the subject assimilates an aspect, property, or attribute of the other and is transformed, wholly or partially, after the model the other provides. It is by means of a series of identifications that the personality is constituted and specified. The roots of the concept can be found in Freud's writings.
Model	Art models are models who pose for photographers, painters, sculptors, and other artists as part of their work of art. Art models are often paid, sometimes even professional, human subjects, who aid in creating a portrait or other work of art including such figure wholly or partially. Models are frequently used for training art students, but are also employed by accomplished artists.
Storytelling	Storytelling is the conveying of events in words, images and sounds, often by improvisation or embellishment. Stories or narratives have been shared in every culture as a means of entertainment, education, cultural preservation and in order to instill moral values. Crucial elements of stories and storytelling include plot, characters and narrative point of view.

Chapter 4. COMMUNICATION

| Shadow | In Jungian psychology, the shadow is a part of the unconscious mind consisting of repressed weaknesses, shortcomings, and instincts. It is one of the three most recognizable archetypes, the others being the anima and animus and the persona. "Everyone carries a shadow," Jung wrote, "and the less it is embodied in the individual's conscious life, the blacker and denser it is." It may be (in part) one's link to more primitive animal instincts, which are superseded during early childhood by the conscious mind. |

Chapter 5. COMMUNICATING EMPATHY: WORKING HARD AT UNDERSTANDING CLIENTS

Empathic accuracy	Empathic accuracy is a term in psychology that refers to how accurately one person (usually designated the perceiver) can infer the thoughts and feelings of another person (usually designated the target). It was first introduced in conjunction with a new research method by psychologists William Ickes and William Tooke in 1988. It is similar to the term accurate empathy, which psychologist Carl Rogers had previously introduced in 1957. Empathic accuracy is an important aspect of what William Ickes has called "everyday mind reading."
	Measurement
	Empathic accuracy became an active topic of psychological research beginning in the 1990s. The impetus for its study was the development by William Ickes and his colleagues of a method to measure the accuracy of a perceiver's inferences about the content of a target person's reported thoughts and feelings.
Pedophilia	As a medical diagnosis, pedophilia is typically defined as a psychiatric disorder in adults or late adolescents (persons age 16 and older) characterized by a primary or exclusive sexual interest in prepubescent children (generally age 13 years or younger, though onset of puberty may vary). The child must be at least five years younger in the case of adolescent pedophiles. The word comes from the Greek: πα?ς (paîs), meaning "child," and φιλ?α (philía), "friendly love" or "friendship", though this literal meaning has been altered toward sexual attraction in modern times, under the titles "child love" or "child lover", by pedophiles who use symbols and codes to identify their preferences.
Assertiveness	Assertiveness is a particular mode of communication. Dorland's Medical Dictionary defines assertiveness as:
	During the second half of the 20th century, assertiveness was increasingly singled out as a behavioral skill taught by many personal development experts, behavior therapists, and cognitive behavioral therapists. Assertiveness is often linked to self-esteem.

Chapter 5. COMMUNICATING EMPATHY: WORKING HARD AT UNDERSTANDING CLIENTS

Communication	Communication is a process whereby meaning is defined and shared between living organisms. Communication requires a sender, a message, and an intended recipient, although the receiver need not be present or aware of the sender's intent to communicate at the time of communication; thus communication can occur across vast distances in time and space. Communication requires that the communicating parties share an area of communicative commonality.
Active	ACTIVE - sobriety, friendship and peace (formerly EGTYF, European Good Templar Youth Federation) is a non-governmental umbrella organisation gathering European youth temperance organisations. ACTIVE is member of the Youth Forum Jeunesse and cooperates with IOGT International. The main aim of Active is peace and tolerance in the world.
Active listening	Active listening is a communication technique that requires the listener to understand, interpret, and evaluate what (s)he hears. The ability to listen actively can improve personal relationships through reducing conflicts, strengthening cooperation, and fostering understanding. When interacting, people often are not listening attentively.
Shadow	In Jungian psychology, the shadow is a part of the unconscious mind consisting of repressed weaknesses, shortcomings, and instincts. It is one of the three most recognizable archetypes, the others being the anima and animus and the persona. "Everyone carries a shadow," Jung wrote, "and the less it is embodied in the individual's conscious life, the blacker and denser it is." It may be (in part) one's link to more primitive animal instincts, which are superseded during early childhood by the conscious mind.
Sensitivity	

The sensitivity, often considered with regard to a particular kind of stimulus, is the strength of the feeling it results in, in comparison with the strength of the stimulus. The concept applies to physical as well as emotional feeling.

Insensitivity

1. Not reacting to the emotions or situation of other people or not caring about others, tactless.
2. Not reacting to something or not appreciating something.
3. Not experiencing physical sensations, numb.

Experience

Experience as a general concept comprises knowledge of or skill in or observation of some thing or some event gained through involvement in or exposure to that thing or event. The history of the word experience aligns it closely with the concept of experiment.

The concept of experience generally refers to know-how or procedural knowledge, rather than propositional knowledge: on-the-job training rather than book-learning.

Bias

In statistics, the term bias refers to several different concepts:

- Selection bias, where individuals or groups are more likely to take part in a research project than others, resulting in biased samples. This can also be termed Berksonian bias.
  - Spectrum bias arises from evaluating diagnostic tests on biased patient samples, leading to an overestimate of the sensitivity and specificity of the test.
- The bias of an estimator is the difference between an estimator's expectation and the true value of the parameter being estimated.

Coping	The psychological definition of coping is the process of managing taxing circumstances, expending effort to solve personal and interpersonal problems, and seeking "to master, minimize, reduce or tolerate stress" or conflict. Coping strategies In coping with stress, people tend to use one of the three main coping strategies: either appraisal-focused, problem-focused, or emotion-focused coping. Appraisal-focused strategies occur when the person modifies the way they think, for example: employing denial, or distancing oneself from the problem.
Facilitation	Facilitation in business, organizational development (OD) and in consensus decision-making refers to the process of designing and running a successful meeting. Facilitation concerns itself with all the tasks needed to run a productive and impartial meeting. Facilitation serves the needs of any group who are meeting with a common purpose, whether it be making a decision, solving a problem, or simply exchanging ideas and information.
Understanding	Understanding is a psychological process related to an abstract or physical object, such as a person, situation, or message whereby one is able to think about it and use concepts to deal adequately with that object. An understanding is the limit of a conceptualization. To understand something is to have conceptualized it to a given measure.

Chapter 5. COMMUNICATING EMPATHY: WORKING HARD AT UNDERSTANDING CLIENTS

Divergent thinking	Divergent thinking is a thought process or method used to generate creative ideas by exploring many possible solutions. It is often used in conjunction with convergent thinking, which follows a particular set of logical steps to arrive at one solution, which in some cases is a "correct" solution. Divergent thinking typically occurs in a spontaneous, free-flowing manner, such that many ideas are generated in an unorganized fashion.
Advice	Advice is a form of relating personal opinions, belief systems, personal values and recommendations about certain situations relayed in some context to another person, group or party often offered as a guide to action and/or conduct. Put a little more simply, an advice message is a recommendation about what might be thought, said, or otherwise done to address a problem, make a decision, or manage a situation. Advice is believed to be theoretical, and is often considered taboo as well as helpful.
Sympathy	Sympathy is a social affinity in which one person stands with another person, closely understanding his or her feelings. Also known as empathic concern, it is the feeling of compassion or concern for another, the wish to see them better off or happier. Although empathy and sympathy are often used interchangeably, a subtle variation in ordinary usage can be detected.

Chapter 6. THE ART OF PROBING AND SUMMARIZING

Professional development	Professional development refers to skills and knowledge attained for both personal development and career advancement. Professional development encompasses all types of facilitated learning opportunities, ranging from college degrees to formal coursework, conferences and informal learning opportunities situated in practice. It has been described as intensive and collaborative, ideally incorporating an evaluative stage There are a variety of approaches to professional development, including consultation, coaching, communities of practice, lesson study, mentoring, reflective supervision and technical assistance.
Curriculum	In formal education, a curriculum is the set of courses, and their content, offered at a school or university. As an idea, curriculum stems from the Latin word for race course, referring to the course of deeds and experiences through which children grow to become mature adults. A curriculum is prescriptive, and is based on a more general syllabus which merely specifies what topics must be understood and to what level to achieve a particular grade or standard.
Decision making	Decision making can be regarded as the mental processes (cognitive process) resulting in the selection of a course of action among several alternatives. Every decision making process produces a final choice. The output can be an action or an opinion of choice.
Exploring	Exploring is a worksite-based program of Learning for Life, a subsidiary of the Boy Scouts of America, for young men and women who are 14 through 20 years old (15 through 21 in some areas). Exploring units, called "posts", usually have a focus on a single career field, such as police, fire/rescue, health, law, aviation, engineering, or the like, and may be sponsored by a government or business entity. Prior to the late 1990s, the Exploring program was the main BSA program for older youth and included posts with an emphasis on outdoor activities, which are now part of the Venturing program.
Active	ACTIVE - sobriety, friendship and peace (formerly EGTYF, European Good Templar Youth Federation) is a non-governmental umbrella organisation gathering European youth temperance organisations. ACTIVE is member of the Youth Forum Jeunesse and cooperates with IOGT International. The main aim of Active is peace and tolerance in the world.
Active listening	Active listening is a communication technique that requires the listener to understand, interpret, and evaluate what (s)he hears. The ability to listen actively can improve personal relationships through reducing conflicts, strengthening cooperation, and fostering understanding.

Chapter 6. THE ART OF PROBING AND SUMMARIZING

When interacting, people often are not listening attentively.

Communication

Communication is a process whereby meaning is defined and shared between living organisms. Communication requires a sender, a message, and an intended recipient, although the receiver need not be present or aware of the sender's intent to communicate at the time of communication; thus communication can occur across vast distances in time and space. Communication requires that the communicating parties share an area of communicative commonality.

Common sense

Common sense, based on a strict construction of the term, consists of what people in common would agree on : that which they "sense" as their common natural understanding. Some people (such as the authors of Merriam-Webster Online) use the phrase to refer to beliefs or propositions that -- in their opinion -- most people would consider prudent and of sound judgment, without reliance on esoteric knowledge or study or research, but based upon what they see as knowledge held by people "in common". Thus "common sense" (in this view) equates to the knowledge and experience which most people already have, or which the person using the term believes that they do or should have.

Empathy

Empathy is the capacity to recognize and, to some extent, share feelings (such as sadness or happiness) that are being experienced by another semi-sentient being. Someone may need to have a certain amount of empathy before they are able to feel compassion.

Etymology

The English word is derived from the Greek word ?μπ?θεια (empatheia), "physical affection, passion, partiality" which comes from ?v (en), "in, at" + π?θος (pathos), "passion" or "suffering".

Flexibility

Flexibility is a personality trait -- the extent to which a person can cope with changes in circumstances and think about problems and tasks in novel, creative ways.

Model

Art models are models who pose for photographers, painters, sculptors, and other artists as part of their work of art. Art models are often paid, sometimes even professional, human subjects, who aid in creating a portrait or other work of art including such figure wholly or partially.

	Models are frequently used for training art students, but are also employed by accomplished artists.
Strategies for Engineered Negligible Senescence	Strategies for Engineered Negligible Senescence is the name Aubrey de Grey gives to his proposal to research regenerative medical procedures to periodically repair all the age-related damage in the human body, thereby maintaining a youthful state indefinitely
	SENS has received media attention but has been criticized by some scientists.
Wisdom	Wisdom is a deep understanding and realizing of people, things, events or situations, resulting in the ability to choose or act to consistently produce the optimum results with a minimum of time and energy. It is the ability to optimally (effectively and efficiently) apply perceptions and knowledge and so produce the desired results. Wisdom is also the comprehension of what is true or right coupled with optimum judgment as to action.

Chapter 7. HELPING CLIENTS CHALLENGE THEMSELVES

Prejudice	A prejudice is a prejudgment, an assumption made about someone or something before having adequate knowledge to be able to do so with guaranteed accuracy. The word prejudice is most commonly used to refer to a preconceived judgment toward a people or a person because of race, social class, gender, ethnicity, homelessness, age, disability, political beliefs, religion, sexual orientation or other personal characteristics. It also means beliefs without knowledge of the facts and may include "any unreasonable attitude that is unusually resistant to rational influence."
Decision making	Decision making can be regarded as the mental processes (cognitive process) resulting in the selection of a course of action among several alternatives. Every decision making process produces a final choice. The output can be an action or an opinion of choice.
Blind spot	A blind spot, is an obscuration of the visual field. A particular blind spot known as the blindspot, or physiological blind spot, or punctum caecum in medical literature is the place in the visual field that corresponds to the lack of light-detecting photoreceptor cells on the optic disc of the retina where the optic nerve passes through it. Since there are no cells to detect light on the optic disc, a part of the field of vision is not perceived.
Egocentrism	In psychology, egocentrism is defined as • the incomplete differentiation of the self and the world, including other people and • the tendency to perceive, understand and interpret the world in terms of the self. An egocentric person cannot fully empathize, i.e. "put himself in other peoples' shoes", and believes everyone sees what she/he sees . It appears that this egocentric stance towards the world is present mostly in younger children.
Therapy	Therapy is the attempted remediation of a health problem, usually following a diagnosis. In the medical field, it is synonymous with the word "treatment". Among psychologists, the term may refer specifically to psychotherapy or "talk therapy".
Emotional expression	In psychology, emotional expression is observable verbal and nonverbal behaviour that communicates emotion. Emotional expression can occur with or without self-awareness. An individual can control such expression, to some extent, and may have deliberate intent in displaying it.

Chapter 7. HELPING CLIENTS CHALLENGE THEMSELVES

Understanding

Understanding is a psychological process related to an abstract or physical object, such as a person, situation, or message whereby one is able to think about it and use concepts to deal adequately with that object.

An understanding is the limit of a conceptualization. To understand something is to have conceptualized it to a given measure.

Emotional intelligence

Emotional intelligence is the ability, capacity, skill; or, in the case of the trait Emotional intelligence model, a self-perceived ability to identify, assess, and control the emotions of oneself, of others, and of groups. Different models have been proposed for the definition of Emotional intelligence and there is disagreement about how the term should be used. Despite these disagreements, which are often highly technical, the ability-Emotional intelligence and trait-Emotional intelligence models (but not the mixed models) enjoy support in the literature and have successful applications in various domains.

Self-Deception

Self-deception is a process of denying or rationalizing away the relevance, significance, or importance of opposing evidence and logical argument. Self-deception involves convincing oneself of a truth (or lack of truth) so that one does not reveal any self-knowledge of the deception.

Definitional problems

A consensus on the identification of self-deception remains elusive to contemporary philosophers, the result of the term's paradoxical elements and ambiguous paradigmatic cases.

Perspective

Perspective, in context of vision and visual perception, is the way in which objects appear to the eye based on their spatial attributes; or their dimensions and the position of the eye relative to the objects. There are two main meanings of the term: linear perspective and aerial perspective.

Linear perspective

As objects become more distant they appear smaller because their visual angle decreases.

Bias	In statistics, the term bias refers to several different concepts: • Selection bias, where individuals or groups are more likely to take part in a research project than others, resulting in biased samples. This can also be termed Berksonian bias. ○ Spectrum bias arises from evaluating diagnostic tests on biased patient samples, leading to an overestimate of the sensitivity and specificity of the test. • The bias of an estimator is the difference between an estimator's expectation and the true value of the parameter being estimated.
Shadow	In Jungian psychology, the shadow is a part of the unconscious mind consisting of repressed weaknesses, shortcomings, and instincts. It is one of the three most recognizable archetypes, the others being the anima and animus and the persona. "Everyone carries a shadow," Jung wrote, "and the less it is embodied in the individual's conscious life, the blacker and denser it is." It may be (in part) one's link to more primitive animal instincts, which are superseded during early childhood by the conscious mind.
Theory	Originally the word theory is a technical term from Ancient Greek. It is derived from theoria, θεωρ? α, meaning "a looking at, viewing, beholding", and refers to contemplation or speculation, as opposed to action. Theory is especially often contrasted to "practice" a concept that in its original Aristotelian context referred to actions done for their own sake, but can also refer to "technical" actions instrumental to some other aim, such as the making of tools or houses.

Chapter 8. CHALLENGING SKILLS AND THE WISDOM TO USE THEM WELL

Hunch	Hunch is a website, designed as a collective intelligence decision-making system that uses decision trees to make decisions based on users' interest. Hunch is building the 'taste graph' for the internet, mapping every person to every entity -- and their affinity for that entity. The system asks users a series of questions about a topic to help weigh the options.
Self-disclosure	Self-disclosure is both the conscious and unconscious act of revealing more about oneself to others. This may include, but is not limited to, thoughts, feelings, aspirations, goals, failures, successes, fears, dreams as well as one's likes, dislikes, and favorites. Typically, a self-disclosure happens when we initially meet someone and continues as we build and develop our relationships with people. As we get to know each other, we disclose information about ourselves. If one person is not willing to "self-disclose" then the other person may stop disclosing information about themselves as well.
Advice	Advice is a form of relating personal opinions, belief systems, personal values and recommendations about certain situations relayed in some context to another person, group or party often offered as a guide to action and/or conduct. Put a little more simply, an advice message is a recommendation about what might be thought, said, or otherwise done to address a problem, make a decision, or manage a situation. Advice is believed to be theoretical, and is often considered taboo as well as helpful.
Motivational interviewing	Motivational interviewing refers to a counseling approach in part developed by clinical psychologists Professor William R Miller, Ph.D. and Professor Stephen Rollnick, Ph.D. It is a client-centered, semi-directive method of engaging intrinsic motivation to change behavior by developing discrepancy and exploring and resolving ambivalence within the client. Motivational interviewing recognizes and accepts the fact that clients who need to make changes in their lives approach counseling at different levels of readiness to change their behavior. If the counseling is mandated, they may never have thought of changing the behavior in question.

Chapter 8. CHALLENGING SKILLS AND THE WISDOM TO USE THEM WELL

Shadow	In Jungian psychology, the shadow is a part of the unconscious mind consisting of repressed weaknesses, shortcomings, and instincts. It is one of the three most recognizable archetypes, the others being the anima and animus and the persona. "Everyone carries a shadow," Jung wrote, "and the less it is embodied in the individual's conscious life, the blacker and denser it is." It may be (in part) one's link to more primitive animal instincts, which are superseded during early childhood by the conscious mind.
Wisdom	Wisdom is a deep understanding and realizing of people, things, events or situations, resulting in the ability to choose or act to consistently produce the optimum results with a minimum of time and energy. It is the ability to optimally (effectively and efficiently) apply perceptions and knowledge and so produce the desired results. Wisdom is also the comprehension of what is true or right coupled with optimum judgment as to action.
Active	ACTIVE - sobriety, friendship and peace (formerly EGTYF, European Good Templar Youth Federation) is a non-governmental umbrella organisation gathering European youth temperance organisations. ACTIVE is member of the Youth Forum Jeunesse and cooperates with IOGT International. The main aim of Active is peace and tolerance in the world.
Active listening	Active listening is a communication technique that requires the listener to understand, interpret, and evaluate what (s)he hears. The ability to listen actively can improve personal relationships through reducing conflicts, strengthening cooperation, and fostering understanding. When interacting, people often are not listening attentively.
Blind spot	A blind spot, is an obscuration of the visual field. A particular blind spot known as the blindspot, or physiological blind spot, or punctum caecum in medical literature is the place in the visual field that corresponds to the lack of light-detecting photoreceptor cells on the optic disc of the retina where the optic nerve passes through it. Since there are no cells to detect light on the optic disc, a part of the field of vision is not perceived.

Bias

In statistics, the term bias refers to several different concepts:

- Selection bias, where individuals or groups are more likely to take part in a research project than others, resulting in biased samples. This can also be termed Berksonian bias.
  - Spectrum bias arises from evaluating diagnostic tests on biased patient samples, leading to an overestimate of the sensitivity and specificity of the test.
- The bias of an estimator is the difference between an estimator's expectation and the true value of the parameter being estimated.

Chapter 9. HELPING DIFFICULT CLIENTS MOVE FORWARD

Resilience	Resilience is the property of a material to absorb energy when it is deformed elastically and then, upon unloading to have this energy recovered. In other words, it is the maximum energy per unit volume that can be elastically stored. It is represented by the area under the curve in the elastic region in the stress-strain curve.
Resistance	"Resistance" as initially used by Sigmund Freud, referred to patients blocking memories from conscious memory. This was a key concept, since the primary treatment method of Freud's talk therapy required making these memories available to the patient's consciousness. "Resistance" expanded Later, Freud described five different forms of resistance.
Active	ACTIVE - sobriety, friendship and peace (formerly EGTYF, European Good Templar Youth Federation) is a non-governmental umbrella organisation gathering European youth temperance organisations. ACTIVE is member of the Youth Forum Jeunesse and cooperates with IOGT International. The main aim of Active is peace and tolerance in the world.
Active listening	Active listening is a communication technique that requires the listener to understand, interpret, and evaluate what (s)he hears. The ability to listen actively can improve personal relationships through reducing conflicts, strengthening cooperation, and fostering understanding. When interacting, people often are not listening attentively.
Fear	Fear is a 1996 thriller film directed by James Foley, starring Mark Wahlberg, Reese Witherspoon, William Petersen, Amy Brenneman and Alyssa Milano. Plot

Nicole Walker (Reese Witherspoon) is a fairly innocent teenager, living with her overbearing father, Steven (William Petersen), her stepmother, Laura (Amy Brenneman), and her stepbrother, Toby (Christopher Gray), but she has a rebellious side particularly directed at Steven. At a rave, she meets David McCall (Mark Wahlberg) and is swept off her feet by his sweet, polite nature.

Intelligence

Intelligence is a term describing a property of the mind including related abilities, such as the capacities for abstract thought, understanding, communication, reasoning, learning, learning from past experiences, planning, and problem solving.

Intelligence is most widely studied in humans, but is also observed in animals and plants. Artificial intelligence is the intelligence of machines or the simulation of intelligence in machines.

Lack

Lack, is, in Lacan's psychoanalytic philosophy, always related to desire. In his seminar Le transfert (1960-61) he states that lack is what causes desire to arise.

However, lack first designated a lack of being: what is desired is being itself.

Hope

Hope is the belief in a positive outcome related to events and circumstances in one's life.

Hope is distinct from positive thinking, which refers to a therapeutic or systematic process used in psychology for reversing pessimism. The term false hope refers to a hope based entirely around a fantasy or an extremely unlikely outcome.

Chapter 9. HELPING DIFFICULT CLIENTS MOVE FORWARD

Shame	Shame is, variously, an affect, emotion, cognition, state, or condition. The roots of the word shame are thought to derive from an older word meaning to cover; as such, covering oneself, literally or figuratively, is a natural expression of shame. Description Nineteenth century scientist Charles Darwin, in his book The Expression of the Emotions in Man and Animals, described shame affect as consisting of blushing, confusion of mind, downward cast eyes, slack posture, and lowered head, and he noted observations of shame affect in human populations worldwide.
Self-disclosure	Self-disclosure is both the conscious and unconscious act of revealing more about oneself to others. This may include, but is not limited to, thoughts, feelings, aspirations, goals, failures, successes, fears, dreams as well as one's likes, dislikes, and favorites. Typically, a self-disclosure happens when we initially meet someone and continues as we build and develop our relationships with people. As we get to know each other, we disclose information about ourselves. If one person is not willing to "self-disclose" then the other person may stop disclosing information about themselves as well.
Strategy	Strategy, a word of military origin, refers to a plan of action designed to achieve a particular goal. In military usage strategy is distinct from tactics, which are concerned with the conduct of an engagement, while strategy is concerned with how different engagements are linked. How a battle is fought is a matter of tactics: the terms and conditions that it is fought on and whether it should be fought at all is a matter of strategy, which is part of the four levels of warfare: political goals or grand strategy, strategy, operations, and tactics.
Reason	In informal logic, a reason consists of either a single premise or co-premises in support of an argument. In formal symbolic logic, only single premises occur. In informal reasoning, two types of reasons exist.
Anonymous	Anonymous is a term used in two senses. As an Internet meme it represents the concept of many on-line community users, or the on-line community itself, acting anonymously in a coordinated manner, usually toward a loosely self-agreed goal. It is generally considered to be a blanket term for members of certain Internet subcultures.

Chapter 9. HELPING DIFFICULT CLIENTS MOVE FORWARD

Flexibility	Flexibility is a personality trait -- the extent to which a person can cope with changes in circumstances and think about problems and tasks in novel, creative ways.
Blind spot	A blind spot, is an obscuration of the visual field. A particular blind spot known as the blindspot, or physiological blind spot, or punctum caecum in medical literature is the place in the visual field that corresponds to the lack of light-detecting photoreceptor cells on the optic disc of the retina where the optic nerve passes through it. Since there are no cells to detect light on the optic disc, a part of the field of vision is not perceived.
Goal setting	Goal setting involves establishing specific, measurable and time-targeted objectives. Goal setting features as a major component of personal development literature. Goals perceived as realistic are more effective in changing behavior.
Model	Art models are models who pose for photographers, painters, sculptors, and other artists as part of their work of art. Art models are often paid, sometimes even professional, human subjects, who aid in creating a portrait or other work of art including such figure wholly or partially. Models are frequently used for training art students, but are also employed by accomplished artists.
Problem solving	Problem solving is a mental process and is part of the larger problem process that includes problem finding and problem shaping. Considered the most complex of all intellectual functions, problem solving has been defined as higher-order cognitive process that requires the modulation and control of more routine or fundamental skills. Problem solving occurs when an organism or an artificial intelligence system needs to move from a given state to a desired goal state.
Coping	The psychological definition of coping is the process of managing taxing circumstances, expending effort to solve personal and interpersonal problems, and seeking "to master, minimize, reduce or tolerate stress" or conflict. Coping strategies

In coping with stress, people tend to use one of the three main coping strategies: either appraisal-focused, problem-focused, or emotion-focused coping.

Appraisal-focused strategies occur when the person modifies the way they think, for example: employing denial, or distancing oneself from the problem.

Coping strategies	The German Freudian psychoanalyst Karen Horney defined four so-called coping strategies to define interpersonal relations, one describing psychologically healthy individuals, the others describing neurotic states.

Moving with

These are the strategies in which psychologically healthy people develop relationships. It involves compromise.

Chapter 10. STAGE I: HELP CLIENTS TELL THEIR STORIES

Model	Art models are models who pose for photographers, painters, sculptors, and other artists as part of their work of art. Art models are often paid, sometimes even professional, human subjects, who aid in creating a portrait or other work of art including such figure wholly or partially. Models are frequently used for training art students, but are also employed by accomplished artists.
Leverage	In statistics, leverage is a term used in connection with regression analysis and, in particular, in analyses aimed at identifying those observations which have a large effect on the outcome of fitting regression models. Leverage points are those observations, if any, made at extreme or outlying values of the independent variables such that the lack of neighbouring observations means that the fitted regression model will pass close to that particular observation. Modern computer packages for statistical analysis include, as part of their facilities for regression analysis, various quantitative measures for identifying influential observations: among these measures is partial leverage, a measure of how a variable contributes to the leverage of a datum.
Self-deception	Self-deception is a process of denying or rationalizing away the relevance, significance, or importance of opposing evidence and logical argument. Self-deception involves convincing oneself of a truth (or lack of truth) so that one does not reveal any self-knowledge of the deception. Definitional problems

A consensus on the identification of self-deception remains elusive to contemporary philosophers, the result of the term's paradoxical elements and ambiguous paradigmatic cases.

Self-disclosure

Self-disclosure is both the conscious and unconscious act of revealing more about oneself to others. This may include, but is not limited to, thoughts, feelings, aspirations, goals, failures, successes, fears, dreams as well as one's likes, dislikes, and favorites.

Typically, a self-disclosure happens when we initially meet someone and continues as we build and develop our relationships with people. As we get to know each other, we disclose information about ourselves. If one person is not willing to "self-disclose" then the other person may stop disclosing information about themselves as well.

Storytelling

Storytelling is the conveying of events in words, images and sounds, often by improvisation or embellishment. Stories or narratives have been shared in every culture as a means of entertainment, education, cultural preservation and in order to instill moral values. Crucial elements of stories and storytelling include plot, characters and narrative point of view.

Fear

Fear is a 1996 thriller film directed by James Foley, starring Mark Wahlberg, Reese Witherspoon, William Petersen, Amy Brenneman and Alyssa Milano.

Plot

Nicole Walker (Reese Witherspoon) is a fairly innocent teenager, living with her overbearing father, Steven (William Petersen), her stepmother, Laura (Amy Brenneman), and her stepbrother, Toby (Christopher Gray), but she has a rebellious side particularly directed at Steven. At a rave, she meets David McCall (Mark Wahlberg) and is swept off her feet by his sweet, polite nature.

Rapport

Rapport is one of the most important features or characteristics of subconscious communication. It is commonality of perspective: being "in sync" with, or being "on the same wavelength" as the person with whom you are talking.

There are a number of techniques that are supposed to be beneficial in building rapport such as: matching your body language (i.e., posture, gesture, etc).; maintaining eye contact; and matching breathing rhythm.

Stress	Stress is a term in psychology and biology, first coined in the biological context in the 1930s, which has in more recent decades become commonly used in popular parlance. It refers to the consequence of the failure of an organism - human or animal - to respond appropriately to emotional or physical threats, whether actual or imagined. Signs of stress may be cognitive, emotional, physical or behavioral.
Exploring	Exploring is a worksite-based program of Learning for Life, a subsidiary of the Boy Scouts of America, for young men and women who are 14 through 20 years old (15 through 21 in some areas). Exploring units, called "posts", usually have a focus on a single career field, such as police, fire/rescue, health, law, aviation, engineering, or the like, and may be sponsored by a government or business entity. Prior to the late 1990s, the Exploring program was the main BSA program for older youth and included posts with an emphasis on outdoor activities, which are now part of the Venturing program.
Learning	Learning is acquiring new or modifying existing knowledge, behaviors, skills, values, or preferences and may involve synthesizing different types of information. The ability to learn is possessed by humans, animals and some machines. Progress over time tends to follow learning curves.
Clinical Psychology	Clinical psychology is an integration of science, theory and clinical knowledge for the purpose of understanding, preventing, and relieving psychologically based distress or dysfunction and to promote subjective well-being and personal development. Central to its practice are psychological assessment and psychological treatment, although clinical psychologists also engage in research, teaching, consultation, forensic testimony, and program development and administration. In many countries, clinical psychology is a regulated mental health profession.

Chapter 10. STAGE I: HELP CLIENTS TELL THEIR STORIES

Journal of Clinical Psychology	The Journal of Clinical Psychology, founded in 1945, is a peer-reviewed forum devoted to psychological research, assessment, and practice. Published eight times a year, the Journal includes research studies; articles on contemporary professional issues, single case research; brief reports (including dissertations in brief); notes from the field; and news and notes. In addition to papers on psychopathology, psychodiagnostics, and the psychotherapeutic process, the journal welcomes articles focusing on psychotherapy effectiveness research, psychological assessment and treatment matching, clinical outcomes, clinical health psychology, and behavioral medicine.
Perspective	Perspective, in context of vision and visual perception, is the way in which objects appear to the eye based on their spatial attributes; or their dimensions and the position of the eye relative to the objects. There are two main meanings of the term: linear perspective and aerial perspective. Linear perspective As objects become more distant they appear smaller because their visual angle decreases.
Active	ACTIVE - sobriety, friendship and peace (formerly EGTYF, European Good Templar Youth Federation) is a non-governmental umbrella organisation gathering European youth temperance organisations. ACTIVE is member of the Youth Forum Jeunesse and cooperates with IOGT International. The main aim of Active is peace and tolerance in the world.
Active listening	Active listening is a communication technique that requires the listener to understand, interpret, and evaluate what (s)he hears. The ability to listen actively can improve personal relationships through reducing conflicts, strengthening cooperation, and fostering understanding. When interacting, people often are not listening attentively.

Chapter 10. STAGE I: HELP CLIENTS TELL THEIR STORIES

Pain	Pain is "an unpleasant sensory and emotional experience associated with actual or potential tissue damage, or described in terms of such damage." It is the feeling common to such experiences as stubbing a toe, burning a finger, putting iodine on a cut, and bumping the "funny bone".
	Pain motivates us to withdraw from potentially damaging situations, protect a damaged body part while it heals, and avoid those situations in the future. Most pain resolves promptly once the painful stimulus is removed and the body has healed, but sometimes pain persists despite removal of the stimulus and apparent healing of the body; and sometimes pain arises in the absence of any detectable stimulus, damage or disease.
Bias	In statistics, the term bias refers to several different concepts: • Selection bias, where individuals or groups are more likely to take part in a research project than others, resulting in biased samples. This can also be termed Berksonian bias. o Spectrum bias arises from evaluating diagnostic tests on biased patient samples, leading to an overestimate of the sensitivity and specificity of the test. • The bias of an estimator is the difference between an estimator's expectation and the true value of the parameter being estimated.
Insight	Insight is the understanding of a specific cause and effect in a specific context. Insight can be used with several related meanings: An insight that manifests itself suddenly, such as understanding how to solve a difficult problem, is sometimes called by the German word Aha-Erlebnis. The term was coined by the German psychologist and theoretical linguist Karl Bühler.

| Shadow | In Jungian psychology, the shadow is a part of the unconscious mind consisting of repressed weaknesses, shortcomings, and instincts. It is one of the three most recognizable archetypes, the others being the anima and animus and the persona. "Everyone carries a shadow," Jung wrote, "and the less it is embodied in the individual's conscious life, the blacker and denser it is." It may be (in part) one's link to more primitive animal instincts, which are superseded during early childhood by the conscious mind. |

Chapter 11. INTRODUCTION TO STAGES II AND III: DECISIONS, GOALS, AND PLANS

Decision making	Decision making can be regarded as the mental processes (cognitive process) resulting in the selection of a course of action among several alternatives. Every decision making process produces a final choice. The output can be an action or an opinion of choice.
Shadow	In Jungian psychology, the shadow is a part of the unconscious mind consisting of repressed weaknesses, shortcomings, and instincts. It is one of the three most recognizable archetypes, the others being the anima and animus and the persona. "Everyone carries a shadow," Jung wrote, "and the less it is embodied in the individual's conscious life, the blacker and denser it is." It may be (in part) one's link to more primitive animal instincts, which are superseded during early childhood by the conscious mind.
Mechanism	Mechanism is the belief that natural wholes (principally living things) are like machines or artifacts, composed of parts lacking any intrinsic relationship to each other, and with their order imposed from without. Thus, the source of an apparent thing's activities is not the whole itself, but its parts or an external influence on the parts. Mechanism is opposed to the organic conception of nature best articulated by Aristotle and more recently elaborated as vitalism.
Discovery	Discovery is the act of detecting something new. With reference to science and academic disciplines, discovery is the observation of new phenomena, new actions, or new events and providing new reasoning to explain the knowledge gathered through such observations with previously acquired knowledge from abstract thought and everyday experiences. Visual discoveries are often called sightings.
Insight	Insight is the understanding of a specific cause and effect in a specific context. Insight can be used with several related meanings: An insight that manifests itself suddenly, such as understanding how to solve a difficult problem, is sometimes called by the German word Aha-Erlebnis. The term was coined by the German psychologist and theoretical linguist Karl Bühler.

Chapter 11. INTRODUCTION TO STAGES II AND III: DECISIONS, GOALS, AND PLANS

Brief therapy	Brief therapy is an umbrella term for a variety of approaches to psychotherapy. It differs from other schools of therapy in that it emphasises (1) a focus on a specific problem and (2) direct intervention. In brief therapy, the therapist takes responsibility for working more pro-actively with the client in order to treat clinical and subjective conditions faster. It also emphasizes precise observation, utilization of natural resources, and temporary suspension of disbelief to consider new perspectives and multiple viewpoints.
Mean	In statistics, mean has two related meanings: • the arithmetic mean (and is distinguished from the geometric mean, which is also called the population mean. There are other statistical measures that use samples that some people confuse with averages - including 'median' and 'mode'. Other simple statistical analyses use measures of spread, such as range, interquartile range, or standard deviation. For a real-valued random variable X, the mean is the expectation of X. Note that not every probability distribution has a defined mean.
Psychotherapy	Psychotherapy is an intentional interpersonal relationship used by trained psychotherapists to aid a client or patient in problems of living. It is a talking therapy and aims to increase the individual's sense of their own well-being. Psychotherapists employ a range of techniques based on experiential relationship building, dialogue, communication and behavior change that are designed to improve the mental health of a client or patient, or to improve group relationships (such as in a family).
Hope	Hope is the belief in a positive outcome related to events and circumstances in one's life. Hope is distinct from positive thinking, which refers to a therapeutic or systematic process used in psychology for reversing pessimism. The term false hope refers to a hope based entirely around a fantasy or an extremely unlikely outcome.

Chapter 11. INTRODUCTION TO STAGES II AND III: DECISIONS, GOALS, AND PLANS

Psychologist	Psychologist is an academic, occupational or professional title used by individuals who are either:

Psychologist is an academic, occupational or professional title used by individuals who are either:

- Social scientists conducting psychological research or teaching psychology in a college or university;
- Academic professionals who apply psychological research, theories and techniques to "real-world" problems, questions and issues in business, industry, or government.
- Clinical professionals who work with patients in a variety of therapeutic contexts (contrast with psychiatrists, who typically provide medical interventions and drug therapies, as opposed to analysis and counseling).

There are many different types of psychologists, as is reflected by the 56 different divisions of the American Psychological Association (APA). Psychologists are generally described as being either "applied" or "research-oriented". The common terms used to describe this central division in psychology are "scientists" or "scholars" (those who conduct research) and "practitioners" or "professionals" (those who apply psychological knowledge).

Chapter 12. STAGE II: HELP CLIENTS SET VIABLE GOALS

Model	Art models are models who pose for photographers, painters, sculptors, and other artists as part of their work of art. Art models are often paid, sometimes even professional, human subjects, who aid in creating a portrait or other work of art including such figure wholly or partially. Models are frequently used for training art students, but are also employed by accomplished artists.
Creativity	Creativity refers to the phenomenon whereby a person creates something new (a product, a solution, a work of art etc). that has some kind of value. What counts as "new" may be in reference to the individual creator, or to the society or domain within which the novelty occurs.
Practice	Practice is the act of rehearsing a behavior over and over, or engaging in an activity again and again, for the purpose of improving or mastering it, as in the phrase "practice makes perfect". Sports teams practice to prepare for actual games. Playing a musical instrument well takes a lot of practice.
Psychotherapy	Psychotherapy is an intentional interpersonal relationship used by trained psychotherapists to aid a client or patient in problems of living. It is a talking therapy and aims to increase the individual's sense of their own well-being. Psychotherapists employ a range of techniques based on experiential relationship building, dialogue, communication and behavior change that are designed to improve the mental health of a client or patient, or to improve group relationships (such as in a family).
Communication	Communication is a process whereby meaning is defined and shared between living organisms. Communication requires a sender, a message, and an intended recipient, although the receiver need not be present or aware of the sender's intent to communicate at the time of communication; thus communication can occur across vast distances in time and space. Communication requires that the communicating parties share an area of communicative commonality.

Chapter 12. STAGE II: HELP CLIENTS SET VIABLE GOALS

Lateral thinking	Lateral thinking is solving problems through an indirect and creative approach, using reasoning that is not immediately obvious and involving ideas that may not be obtainable by using only traditional step-by-step logic. The term lateral thinking was coined by Edward de Bono in the book New Think: The Use of Lateral Thinking published in 1967. Methods Critical thinking is primarily concerned with judging the true value of statements and seeking errors.
Therapeutic relationship	The therapeutic relationship, the therapeutic alliance, and the working alliance, refers to the relationship between a healthcare professional and a client (or patient). It is the means by which the professional hopes to engage with, and affect change in a client. Research While much early work on this subject was generated from a psychodynamic perspective, researchers from other orientations have since investigated this area.
Brainstorming	Brainstorming is a group creativity technique designed to generate a large number of ideas for the solution of a problem. In 1953 the method was popularized by Alex Faickney Osborn in a book called Applied Imagination. Osborn proposed that groups could double their creative output with brainstorming.
Divergent thinking	Divergent thinking is a thought process or method used to generate creative ideas by exploring many possible solutions. It is often used in conjunction with convergent thinking, which follows a particular set of logical steps to arrive at one solution, which in some cases is a "correct" solution. Divergent thinking typically occurs in a spontaneous, free-flowing manner, such that many ideas are generated in an unorganized fashion.
Exemplar	Exemplar, in the sense developed by philosopher of science Thomas Kuhn, is a well known usage of a scientific theory.

According to Kuhn, scientific practice alternates between periods of normal science and extraordinary/revolutionary science. During periods of normalcy, scientists tend to subscribe to a large body of interconnecting knowledge, methods, and assumptions which make up the reigning paradigm .

Exploring

Exploring is a worksite-based program of Learning for Life, a subsidiary of the Boy Scouts of America, for young men and women who are 14 through 20 years old (15 through 21 in some areas). Exploring units, called "posts", usually have a focus on a single career field, such as police, fire/rescue, health, law, aviation, engineering, or the like, and may be sponsored by a government or business entity. Prior to the late 1990s, the Exploring program was the main BSA program for older youth and included posts with an emphasis on outdoor activities, which are now part of the Venturing program.

Brief therapy

Brief therapy is an umbrella term for a variety of approaches to psychotherapy. It differs from other schools of therapy in that it emphasises (1) a focus on a specific problem and (2) direct intervention. In brief therapy, the therapist takes responsibility for working more pro-actively with the client in order to treat clinical and subjective conditions faster. It also emphasizes precise observation, utilization of natural resources, and temporary suspension of disbelief to consider new perspectives and multiple viewpoints.

Intention

In criminal law, intention is one of the three general classes of mens rea necessary to constitute a conventional as opposed to strict liability crime.

Definitions

Intention is defined in R. v Mohan as "the decision to bring about a prohibited consequence".

A range of words is used to represent shades of intention in the various criminal laws around the world.

Goal setting

Goal setting involves establishing specific, measurable and time-targeted objectives. Goal setting features as a major component of personal development literature. Goals perceived as realistic are more effective in changing behavior.

Chapter 12. STAGE II: HELP CLIENTS SET VIABLE GOALS

Frame	The Frame refers to the environment and relationship in psychotherapy, which enables the client to be open about their life with the therapist, in a secure and confidential manner. It is one of the most important elements in psychotherapy and counselling.
	Significance
	Success in psychotherapy and counselling has been associated with the therapeutic relationship between the client and the therapist.
Self-deception	Self-deception is a process of denying or rationalizing away the relevance, significance, or importance of opposing evidence and logical argument. Self-deception involves convincing oneself of a truth (or lack of truth) so that one does not reveal any self-knowledge of the deception.
	Definitional problems
	A consensus on the identification of self-deception remains elusive to contemporary philosophers, the result of the term's paradoxical elements and ambiguous paradigmatic cases.
Self-disclosure	Self-disclosure is both the conscious and unconscious act of revealing more about oneself to others. This may include, but is not limited to, thoughts, feelings, aspirations, goals, failures, successes, fears, dreams as well as one's likes, dislikes, and favorites.
	Typically, a self-disclosure happens when we initially meet someone and continues as we build and develop our relationships with people. As we get to know each other, we disclose information about ourselves. If one person is not willing to "self-disclose" then the other person may stop disclosing information about themselves as well.

Bias	In statistics, the term bias refers to several different concepts: • Selection bias, where individuals or groups are more likely to take part in a research project than others, resulting in biased samples. This can also be termed Berksonian bias. o Spectrum bias arises from evaluating diagnostic tests on biased patient samples, leading to an overestimate of the sensitivity and specificity of the test. • The bias of an estimator is the difference between an estimator's expectation and the true value of the parameter being estimated.
Coercion	Coercion is the practice of forcing another party to behave in an involuntary manner (whether through action or inaction) by use of threats,or rewards intimidation or some other form of pressure or force. Such actions are used as leverage, to force the victim to act in the desired way. Coercion may involve the actual infliction of physical pain/injury or psychological harm in order to enhance the credibility of a threat.
Cognitive dissonance	Cognitive dissonance is an uncomfortable feeling caused by holding conflicting ideas simultaneously. The theory of cognitive dissonance proposes that people have a motivational drive to reduce dissonance. They do this by changing their attitudes, beliefs, and actions.
Cognitive psychology	Cognitive psychology is a subdiscipline of psychology exploring internal mental processes. It is the study of how people perceive, remember, think, speak, and solve problems. Cognitive psychology is radically different from previous psychological approaches in two key ways.
Affect	"Affect" is a concept used in philosophy by Spinoza, Deleuze and Guattari. According to Spinoza's Ethics III, 3, Definition 3, an affect is an empowerment, and not a simple change or modification. Affects, according to Deleuze, are not simple affections, as they are independent from their subject.
Agenda	An agenda is a list of meeting activities in the order in which they are to be taken up, beginning with the call to order and ending with adjournment. It usually includes one or more specific items of business to be considered. It may, but is not required to, include specific times for one OR more activities.

Chapter 12. STAGE II: HELP CLIENTS SET VIABLE GOALS

Self-efficacy	Self-efficacy has been defined in a variety of ways: as the belief that one is capable of performing in a certain manner to attain certain goals, as a person's belief about their capabilities to produce designated levels of performance that exercise influence over events that affect their lives. It is a belief that one has the capabilities to execute the courses of actions required to manage prospective situations. It has been described in other ways as the concept has evolved in the literature and in society: as the sense of belief that one's actions have an effect on the environment; as a person's judgment of his or her capabilities based on mastery criteria; a sense of a person's competence within a specific framework, focusing on the person's assessment of their abilities to perform specific tasks in relation to goals and standards rather than in comparison with others' capabilities.
Resilience	Resilience is the property of a material to absorb energy when it is deformed elastically and then, upon unloading to have this energy recovered. In other words, it is the maximum energy per unit volume that can be elastically stored. It is represented by the area under the curve in the elastic region in the stress-strain curve.
Positive feedback	A system exhibiting positive feedback, in response to perturbation, acts to increase the magnitude of the perturbation. That is, "A produces more of B which in turn produces more of A". In contrast, a system that responds to a perturbation in a way that reduces its effect is said to exhibit negative feedback. These concepts were first recognized as broadly applicable by Norbert Wiener in his 1948 work on cybernetics.
Anxiety	Anxiety is a psychological and physiological state characterized by somatic, emotional, cognitive, and behavioral components. The root meaning of the word anxiety is 'to vex or trouble'; in either the absence or presence of psychological stress, anxiety can create feelings of fear, worry, uneasiness and dread. Anxiety is considered to be a normal reaction to stress.
Fear	Fear is a 1996 thriller film directed by James Foley, starring Mark Wahlberg, Reese Witherspoon, William Petersen, Amy Brenneman and Alyssa Milano. Plot Nicole Walker (Reese Witherspoon) is a fairly innocent teenager, living with her overbearing father, Steven (William Petersen), her stepmother, Laura (Amy Brenneman), and her stepbrother, Toby (Christopher Gray), but she has a rebellious side particularly directed at Steven. At a rave, she meets David McCall (Mark Wahlberg) and is swept off her feet by his sweet, polite nature.

| Decision making | Decision making can be regarded as the mental processes (cognitive process) resulting in the selection of a course of action among several alternatives. Every decision making process produces a final choice. The output can be an action or an opinion of choice. |

Chapter 13. STAGE III

Model	Art models are models who pose for photographers, painters, sculptors, and other artists as part of their work of art. Art models are often paid, sometimes even professional, human subjects, who aid in creating a portrait or other work of art including such figure wholly or partially. Models are frequently used for training art students, but are also employed by accomplished artists.
Shadow	In Jungian psychology, the shadow is a part of the unconscious mind consisting of repressed weaknesses, shortcomings, and instincts. It is one of the three most recognizable archetypes, the others being the anima and animus and the persona. "Everyone carries a shadow," Jung wrote, "and the less it is embodied in the individual's conscious life, the blacker and denser it is." It may be (in part) one's link to more primitive animal instincts, which are superseded during early childhood by the conscious mind.
Brainstorming	Brainstorming is a group creativity technique designed to generate a large number of ideas for the solution of a problem. In 1953 the method was popularized by Alex Faickney Osborn in a book called Applied Imagination. Osborn proposed that groups could double their creative output with brainstorming.
Communication	Communication is a process whereby meaning is defined and shared between living organisms. Communication requires a sender, a message, and an intended recipient, although the receiver need not be present or aware of the sender's intent to communicate at the time of communication; thus communication can occur across vast distances in time and space. Communication requires that the communicating parties share an area of communicative commonality.
Therapeutic relationship	The therapeutic relationship, the therapeutic alliance, and the working alliance, refers to the relationship between a healthcare professional and a client (or patient). It is the means by which the professional hopes to engage with, and affect change in a client. Research

While much early work on this subject was generated from a psychodynamic perspective, researchers from other orientations have since investigated this area.

Divergent thinking	Divergent thinking is a thought process or method used to generate creative ideas by exploring many possible solutions. It is often used in conjunction with convergent thinking, which follows a particular set of logical steps to arrive at one solution, which in some cases is a "correct" solution. Divergent thinking typically occurs in a spontaneous, free-flowing manner, such that many ideas are generated in an unorganized fashion.
Therapy	Therapy is the attempted remediation of a health problem, usually following a diagnosis. In the medical field, it is synonymous with the word "treatment". Among psychologists, the term may refer specifically to psychotherapy or "talk therapy".
Life skills	Life skills are a set of human skills acquired via teaching or direct experience that are used to handle problems and questions commonly encountered in daily human life.
Belief	Belief is the psychological state in which an individual holds a proposition or premise to be true.
	Belief, knowledge and epistemology
	The terms belief and knowledge are used differently in philosophy.
	Epistemology is the philosophical study of knowledge and belief.
Procedure	A procedure is a specified series of actions or operations which have to be executed in the same manner in order to always obtain the same result under the same circumstances (for example, emergency procedures). Less precisely speaking, this word can indicate a sequence of tasks, steps, decisions, calculations and processes, that when undertaken in the sequence laid down produces the described result, product or outcome. A procedure usually induces a change.

Chapter 13. STAGE III

Sampling	Sampling is that part of statistical practice concerned with the selection of a subset of individual observations within a population of individuals intended to yield some knowledge about the population of concern, especially for the purposes of making predictions based on statistical inference. Researchers rarely survey the entire population for two reasons (Adèr, Mellenbergh, ' Hand, 2008): the cost is too high, and the population is dynamic in that the individuals making up the population may change over time. The three main advantages of sampling are that the cost is lower, data collection is faster, and since the data set is smaller it is possible to ensure homogeneity and to improve the accuracy and quality of the data.
Balance	In biomechanics, balance is an ability to maintain the center of gravity of a body within the base of support with minimal postural sway. When exercising the ability to balance, one is said to be balancing. Balancing requires concurrent processing of inputs from multiple senses, including equilibrioception (from the vestibular system), vision, and perception of pressure and proprioception (from the somatosensory system), while the motor system simultaneously controls muscle actions.
Self-efficacy	Self-efficacy has been defined in a variety of ways: as the belief that one is capable of performing in a certain manner to attain certain goals, as a person's belief about their capabilities to produce designated levels of performance that exercise influence over events that affect their lives. It is a belief that one has the capabilities to execute the courses of actions required to manage prospective situations. It has been described in other ways as the concept has evolved in the literature and in society: as the sense of belief that one's actions have an effect on the environment; as a person's judgment of his or her capabilities based on mastery criteria; a sense of a person's competence within a specific framework, focusing on the person's assessment of their abilities to perform specific tasks in relation to goals and standards rather than in comparison with others' capabilities.

Chapter 13. STAGE III

Wishful thinking	Wishful thinking is the formation of beliefs and making decisions according to what might be pleasing to imagine instead of by appealing to evidence, rationality or reality. Studies have consistently shown that holding all else equal, subjects will predict positive outcomes to be more likely than negative outcomes . Notable examples Prominent examples of wishful thinking include: • Economist Irving Fisher said that "stock prices have reached what looks like a permanently high plateau" a few weeks before the Stock Market Crash of 1929, which was followed by the Great Depression. • President John F. Kennedy believed that, if overpowered by Cuban forces, the CIA-backed rebels could "escape destruction by melting into the countryside" in the Bay of Pigs Invasion. As a logical fallacy In addition to being a cognitive bias and a poor way of making decisions, wishful thinking is commonly held to be a specific logical fallacy in an argument when it is assumed that because we wish something to be true or false that it is actually true or false.
Hypothetico-deductive model	The hypothetico-deductive model, first so-named by William Whewell, is a proposed description of scientific method. According to it, scientific inquiry proceeds by formulating a hypothesis in a form that could conceivably be falsified by a test on observable data. A test that could and does run contrary to predictions of the hypothesis is taken as a falsification of the hypothesis.
Discipline	In its most general sense, discipline refers to systematic instruction given to a disciple. it is also known as sesencd witch means seasons or tempritrue. To discipline son to follow a particular code of conduct or "order".

Chapter 13. STAGE III

Active	ACTIVE - sobriety, friendship and peace (formerly EGTYF, European Good Templar Youth Federation) is a non-governmental umbrella organisation gathering European youth temperance organisations. ACTIVE is member of the Youth Forum Jeunesse and cooperates with IOGT International. The main aim of Active is peace and tolerance in the world.
Resilience	Resilience is the property of a material to absorb energy when it is deformed elastically and then, upon unloading to have this energy recovered. In other words, it is the maximum energy per unit volume that can be elastically stored. It is represented by the area under the curve in the elastic region in the stress-strain curve.
Lack	Lack, is, in Lacan's psychoanalytic philosophy, always related to desire. In his seminar Le transfert (1960-61) he states that lack is what causes desire to arise. However, lack first designated a lack of being: what is desired is being itself.
Anonymous	Anonymous is a term used in two senses. As an Internet meme it represents the concept of many on-line community users, or the on-line community itself, acting anonymously in a coordinated manner, usually toward a loosely self-agreed goal. It is generally considered to be a blanket term for members of certain Internet subcultures.
Systematic desensitization	Systematic desensitization is a type of behavioral therapy used in the field of psychology to help effectively overcome phobias and other anxiety disorders. More specifically, it is a type of Pavlovian therapy / classical conditioning therapy developed by a South African psychiatrist, Joseph Wolpe. To begin the process of systematic desensitization, one must first be taught relaxation skills in order to extinguish fear and anxiety responses to specific phobias.
Active listening	Active listening is a communication technique that requires the listener to understand, interpret, and evaluate what (s)he hears. The ability to listen actively can improve personal relationships through reducing conflicts, strengthening cooperation, and fostering understanding.

When interacting, people often are not listening attentively.

Practice	Practice is the act of rehearsing a behavior over and over, or engaging in an activity again and again, for the purpose of improving or mastering it, as in the phrase "practice makes perfect". Sports teams practice to prepare for actual games. Playing a musical instrument well takes a lot of practice.
Psychotherapy	Psychotherapy is an intentional interpersonal relationship used by trained psychotherapists to aid a client or patient in problems of living.
	It is a talking therapy and aims to increase the individual's sense of their own well-being. Psychotherapists employ a range of techniques based on experiential relationship building, dialogue, communication and behavior change that are designed to improve the mental health of a client or patient, or to improve group relationships (such as in a family).
Shaping	The differential reinforcement of successive approximations, or more commonly, shaping is a conditioning procedure used primarily in the experimental analysis of behavior. It was introduced by B.F. Skinner with pigeons and extended to dogs, dolphins, humans and other species. In shaping, the form of an existing response is gradually changed across successive trials towards a desired target behavior by rewarding exact segments of behavior.
Clinical Psychology	Clinical psychology is an integration of science, theory and clinical knowledge for the purpose of understanding, preventing, and relieving psychologically based distress or dysfunction and to promote subjective well-being and personal development. Central to its practice are psychological assessment and psychological treatment, although clinical psychologists also engage in research, teaching, consultation, forensic testimony, and program development and administration. In many countries, clinical psychology is a regulated mental health profession.

Chapter 13. STAGE III

Consulting	Consulting is providing advice in a particular area of expertise. This is not the same as customer service. Specific types of consulting include: • Professional Engineering Various Disciplines • Management consulting • Medicine • Biotechnology consulting • Environmental consulting • Faculty consulting • Franchise consulting • Human resource consulting • Information technology consulting • Performance consulting • Political consulting • Supply chain consulting • Trial consulting .
Evidence-based practice	The term evidence-based practice or empirically-supported treatment (EST) refers to preferential use of mental and behavioral health interventions for which systematic empirical research has provided evidence of statistically significant effectiveness as treatments for specific problems. In recent years, Evidence based practice has been stressed by professional organizations such as the American Psychological Association, the American Occupational Therapy Association, the American Nurses Association, and the American Physical Therapy Association, which have also strongly recommended their members to carry out investigations to provide evidence supporting or rejecting the use of specific interventions. Equivalent recommendations apply to the Canadian equivalent of these associations.
Science	Science is an enterprise that builds and organizes knowledge in the form of testable explanations and predictions about the world. An older meaning still in use today is that of Aristotle, for whom scientific knowledge was a body of reliable knowledge that can be logically and rationally explained . Since classical antiquity science as a type of knowledge was closely linked to philosophy.

Psychologist

Psychologist is an academic, occupational or professional title used by individuals who are either:

- Social scientists conducting psychological research or teaching psychology in a college or university;
- Academic professionals who apply psychological research, theories and techniques to "real-world" problems, questions and issues in business, industry, or government.
- Clinical professionals who work with patients in a variety of therapeutic contexts (contrast with psychiatrists, who typically provide medical interventions and drug therapies, as opposed to analysis and counseling).

There are many different types of psychologists, as is reflected by the 56 different divisions of the American Psychological Association (APA). Psychologists are generally described as being either "applied" or "research-oriented". The common terms used to describe this central division in psychology are "scientists" or "scholars" (those who conduct research) and "practitioners" or "professionals" (those who apply psychological knowledge).

Chapter 14. GETTING THERE

Discipline	In its most general sense, discipline refers to systematic instruction given to a disciple. it is also known as sesencd witch means seasons or tempritrue. To discipline son to follow a particular code of conduct or "order".
Bias	In statistics, the term bias refers to several different concepts: • Selection bias, where individuals or groups are more likely to take part in a research project than others, resulting in biased samples. This can also be termed Berksonian bias. o Spectrum bias arises from evaluating diagnostic tests on biased patient samples, leading to an overestimate of the sensitivity and specificity of the test. • The bias of an estimator is the difference between an estimator's expectation and the true value of the parameter being estimated.
Intention	In criminal law, intention is one of the three general classes of mens rea necessary to constitute a conventional as opposed to strict liability crime. Definitions Intention is defined in R. v Mohan as "the decision to bring about a prohibited consequence". A range of words is used to represent shades of intention in the various criminal laws around the world.
Procrastination	In psychology, procrastination refers to the act of replacing high-priority actions with tasks of low-priority, and thus putting off important tasks to a later time. Psychologists often cite such behavior as a mechanism for coping with the anxiety associated with starting or completing any task or decision. Schraw, Pinard, Wadkins, and Olafson have proposed three criteria for a behavior to be classified as procrastination: it must be counterproductive, needless, and delaying.

Chapter 14. GETTING THERE

Incentive	In economics and sociology, an incentive is any factor (financial or non-financial) that enables or motivates a particular course of action, or counts as a reason for preferring one choice to the alternatives. It is an expectation that encourages people to behave in a certain way. Since human beings are purposeful creatures, the study of incentive structures is central to the study of all economic activity (both in terms of individual decision-making and in terms of co-operation and competition within a larger institutional structure).
Extinction	Extinction is the conditioning phenomenon in which a previously learned response to a cue is reduced when the cue is presented in the absence of the previously paired aversive or appetitive stimulus. Fear conditioning Extinction is typically studied within the Pavlovian fear conditioning framework in which extinction refers to the reduction in a conditioned response (CR; e.g., fear response/freezing) when a conditioned stimulus (CS; e.g., neutral stimulus/light or tone) is repeatedly presented in the absence of the unconditioned stimulus (US; e.g., foot shock/loud noise) with which it has been previously paired. The simplest explanation of extinction is that as the CS is presented without the aversive US, the animal gradually "unlearns" the CS-US association which is known as the associative loss theory.
Social network	A social network is a social structure made up of individuals (or organizations) called "nodes", which are tied (connected) by one or more specific types of interdependency, such as friendship, kinship, common interest, financial exchange, dislike, sexual relationships, or relationships of beliefs, knowledge or prestige. Social network analysis views social relationships in terms of network theory consisting of nodes and ties (also called edges, links, or connections). Nodes are the individual actors within the networks, and ties are the relationships between the actors.

Chapter 14. GETTING THERE

Shadow	In Jungian psychology, the shadow is a part of the unconscious mind consisting of repressed weaknesses, shortcomings, and instincts. It is one of the three most recognizable archetypes, the others being the anima and animus and the persona. "Everyone carries a shadow," Jung wrote, "and the less it is embodied in the individual's conscious life, the blacker and denser it is." It may be (in part) one's link to more primitive animal instincts, which are superseded during early childhood by the conscious mind.
Learned helplessness	Learned helplessness, as a technical term in animal psychology and related human psychology, means a condition of a human being or an animal in which it has learned to behave helplessly, even when the opportunity is restored for it to help itself by avoiding an unpleasant or harmful circumstance to which it has been subjected. Learned helplessness theory is the view that clinical depression and related mental illnesses may result from a perceived absence of control over the outcome of a situation.
	Foundation of research and theory
	Seligman and Maier
	The American psychologist Martin Seligman's foundational experiments and theory of learned helplessness began at University of Pennsylvania in 1967, as an extension of his interest in depression.
Learned optimism	Learned optimism is the idea in positive psychology that a talent for joy, like any other, can be cultivated. It is contrasted with learned helplessness. Learning optimism is done by consciously challenging any negative self talk.
Optimism	The Oxford English Dictionary defines optimism as having "hopefulness and confidence about the future or successful outcome of something; a tendency to take a favourable or hopeful view." The word is originally derived from the Latin optimum, meaning "best." Unlike optimal thinking, which is realistic in nature, being optimistic, in the typical sense of the word, ultimately means one expects the best possible outcome from any given situation. This is usually referred to in psychology as dispositional optimism. Researchers sometimes operationalize the term differently depending on their research, however.

Chapter 14. GETTING THERE

Self-disclosure	Self-disclosure is both the conscious and unconscious act of revealing more about oneself to others. This may include, but is not limited to, thoughts, feelings, aspirations, goals, failures, successes, fears, dreams as well as one's likes, dislikes, and favorites. Typically, a self-disclosure happens when we initially meet someone and continues as we build and develop our relationships with people. As we get to know each other, we disclose information about ourselves. If one person is not willing to "self-disclose" then the other person may stop disclosing information about themselves as well.
Empowerment	Empowerment refers to increasing the spiritual, political, social, or economic strength of individuals and communities. It often involves the empowered developing confidence in their own capacities.
Entropy	In information theory, entropy is a measure of the uncertainty associated with a random variable. In this context, the term usually refers to the Shannon entropy, which quantifies the expected value of the information contained in a message, usually in units such as bits. Equivalently, the Shannon entropy is a measure of the average information content one is missing when one does not know the value of the random variable.
Fear	Fear is a 1996 thriller film directed by James Foley, starring Mark Wahlberg, Reese Witherspoon, William Petersen, Amy Brenneman and Alyssa Milano. Plot Nicole Walker (Reese Witherspoon) is a fairly innocent teenager, living with her overbearing father, Steven (William Petersen), her stepmother, Laura (Amy Brenneman), and her stepbrother, Toby (Christopher Gray), but she has a rebellious side particularly directed at Steven. At a rave, she meets David McCall (Mark Wahlberg) and is swept off her feet by his sweet, polite nature.
Hope	Hope is the belief in a positive outcome related to events and circumstances in one's life.

Hope is distinct from positive thinking, which refers to a therapeutic or systematic process used in psychology for reversing pessimism. The term false hope refers to a hope based entirely around a fantasy or an extremely unlikely outcome.

| Storytelling | Storytelling is the conveying of events in words, images and sounds, often by improvisation or embellishment. Stories or narratives have been shared in every culture as a means of entertainment, education, cultural preservation and in order to instill moral values. Crucial elements of stories and storytelling include plot, characters and narrative point of view. |

Lightning Source UK Ltd.
Milton Keynes UK
UKHW052012111218
333848UK00003BA/178/P